PRAISE FOR *EVERYBODY'S BUSINESS*

"Wilson's expertise in transformational leadership shines through in this pioneering work. The notable tips she offers and the questions for reflection in each chapter will assist you in discovering the first easy steps you can take toward sustainable high performance."

—Jim MacDonald, Vice President of Human Resources—Americas, Hilton Worldwide

"Through micro vignettes, startlingly clear insights, and a wealth of knowledge drawn from customer-based experiences, *Everybody's Business* demonstrates how organizations large and small, public and private, can ignite their corporate 'imaginative moxie' to cultivate the dormant seeds of leadership buried within their employees and steer their organizations to greatness, 'one decision, one action, and one person at a time.'"

—Major General Barry D. Bates (USA, Retired), Vice President of Operations, National Defense Industrial Association

"*Everybody's Business* is a must-read for everyone in business. Its core message that successful leaders seek input is elegant but simple. This well-written book changed my thinking of how to gather data critical to our strategic success."

—Gary Shapiro, President and CEO of the Consumer Electronics Association (CEA)

"*Everybody's Business* provides a modern, practical approach to inspiring enterprise growth through true collaboration. Wilson applies her practical wisdom anchored by 'chats' with experts to help you transform your enterprise in ways that are leaner, faster, better, and smarter. You'll refer to this book again and again."

—Maria Proestou, President of DELTA Resources, Inc.

"*Everybody's Business* is a must-read as we discover what it means to do business in the new economy and how to create conscious, high-performing organizations. The memorable insights Wilson shares and the 'Ask Yourself' section in each chapter help you determine small actions that yield big returns."

—Craig A. Parisot, Chief Operating Officer of Invertix Corporation

"*Everybody's Business* is an outstanding primer on what really matters in complex organizations. It is a compelling tale, utilizing very specific examples on why culture and leadership matter so much to the success of a business. Dr. Marta Wilson has crafted an easy-to-read book on exactly how and what both new and seasoned executives need to pay attention to in order to gain the most success for their people. At the heart of the book, similar to the golden rule of real estate which is "location, location, location," it's about your "people, people, people." Wilson's original take on leadership and stakeholder engagement will inspire you to think differently and empower you to take the next step to create improvement within your enterprise. Get ready to imagine new possibilities and bring them into reality in your workplace!"

—Rear Admiral Jim McManamon (USN, Retired),
former Deputy Commander of Surface Warfare, Naval Sea Systems Command

EVERYBODY'S
BUSINESS

EVERYBODY'S
BUSINESS

Engaging Your Total Enterprise *to* Boost
Quality, Speed, Savings *and* Innovation

DR. MARTA WILSON
Featuring Dr. Altyn Clark and Colleagues

GREENLEAF
BOOK GROUP PRESS

Published by Greenleaf Book Group Press
Austin, Texas
www.gbgpress.com

Distributed by Greenleaf Book Group LLC

For ordering information or special discounts for bulk purchases, please contact Greenleaf Book Group LLC at PO Box 91869, Austin, TX 78709, 512.891.6100.

Design and composition by Greenleaf Book Group LLC
Cover design by Greenleaf Book Group LLC

Publisher's Cataloging-In-Publication Data
(Prepared by The Donohue Group, Inc.)

Wilson, M. C. (Marta C.), 1963-
   Everybody's business : engaging your total enterprise to boost quality, speed, savings and innovation / Marta Wilson ; featuring Altyn Clark and colleagues. -- 1st ed.

   p. ; cm.

   Issued also as an ebook.
   ISBN: 978-1-60832-392-0

   1. Labor productivity. 2. Communication in organizations. 3. Management--Employee participation. 4. Organizational learning. I. Clark, Altyn. II. Title.

HD57 .W55 2012
658.314   2012935213

Part of the Tree Neutral® program, which offsets the number of trees consumed in the production and printing of this book by taking proactive steps, such as planting trees in direct proportion to the number of trees used: www.treeneutral.com

TreeNeutral®

Printed in the United States of America on acid-free paper

12 13 14   10 9 8 7 6 5 4 3 2 1

First Edition

This book is dedicated to Dr. Roseanne Foti. Thank you for igniting the launch of my professional flight and the flights of so many others you've mentored. You are a role model and an inspiration to all who know and love you.

CONTENTS

EXPERTS

This book features insights from eight dear colleagues and thought leaders:

Altyn Clark, PhD, PE
Brian Skimmons, MSTM, PMP
Garry Coleman, PhD, PE
Patrick Hartman, PhD, PE
Paul Odomirok, MEd, LSSMBB
Sharon Flinder, PhD
Vaughan Limbrick, MS, HCS
William Bracken, PhD

ACKNOWLEDGMENTS

There are many possibility thinkers and thought leaders whom I wish to thank for their contributions to this book. In particular, these esteemed colleagues and inspiring mentors include Dr. William Bracken, Dr. Altyn Clark, Dr. Garry Coleman, Dr. Sharon Flinder, Dr. Patrick Hartman, Ms. Vaughan Limbrick, Mr. Paul Odomirok, and Mr. Brian Skimmons.

I have drawn great ideas from a remarkable lineup of industry titans, including those invited to speak before the Northern Virginia Technology Council, which is the largest technology business association in the country. Other leaders in the regional exchange of ideas to whom I express gratitude are the Armed Forces Communications and Electronics Association, Inc. 5000, the National Defense Industrial Association, the

Professional Services Council, the Small and Emerging Contractors Advisory Forum, the Society for Human Resource Management, the Marine Corps Association, the Virginia Chamber of Commerce, and the *Washington Business Journal.*

For uplifting stories of selfless courage that inspire us all, I thank the following charitable organizations: Equal Footing Foundation, Marine Toys for Tots Foundation, So Others Might Eat, various wounded warrior organizations, and the March of Dimes. As part of TSI's corporate social responsibility initiate, we invest time, energy, and resources to support their missions.

Nicole Thompson, scholar-researcher, served as a graduate intern for two years, contributing to the body of knowledge on which this work rests. Janelle Millard, strategic communications manager, is one of the bright lights at TSI, where she has become an indispensable associate serving the community at large. Without them both, I would not have been able to produce this work while running a vibrant company.

Before closing, I'm particularly delighted to acknowledge the signature professionalism of TSI's talented employees, stellar teaming partners, committed service providers, and dedicated customers within the defense and national security communities.

On a personal note, as always, I express special thanks to my husband and sailing companion, Bob Wilson, for joining me on this remarkable journey.

PREFACE

Are you ready to move forward? This book is about the next best step to be made by someone—anyone—in your organization. It can be a very small step and yet have a measurably powerful impact on productivity and profit. This book gives you a new confidence that small possibilities with big outcomes are waiting to be found in your organization— right now.

A serendipitous collection of favorite ideas that have sparked the imagination and success of our customers over the years, this book will energize your bold goals and your vision of the future. My wish is that one or two of these ideas might revitalize your own innovative confidence. You can consider this book a thought provocateur. It's not food for thought; instead, it contains seeds for thinking—about your own enterprise. You need to take it from there.

Most leaders these days run short, at some point, on imaginative moxie. Have you? Let's do a quick test: Do you know how to build agility into your enterprise, no matter how big or how lumbering it has been to date? If not, you need imaginative revitalization, because these days, agility is synonymous with longevity.

I'm here to remind you that you can sustain longevity by imagining the smallest step with the biggest payoff and then choosing that one step in lieu of all other options. Even better, I can help you imagine ways to free everybody connected to your organization to do the same: to make it *everybody's business* to know and grow your enterprise!

This book is based on research and practice. However, like most instigators of bold possibility thinking, it doesn't talk much about either. Instead, it focuses on opportunities, actions, and results.

These pages cast a spotlight on what happens after the latest research and possibility thinking have been incorporated into time-tested methods. The object is to help you focus on the open question remaining when smarts and talent tackle a problem. Are people really working, producing and serving in ways that are leaner, faster, better, and smarter? Do you know how to know if they are?

Most importantly, how can you know, before launching a change to create improvement, whether it's the right change or improvement? How do you contend with the haunting reality of opportunity costs?

Some leaders in small businesses, large corporations, government agencies, and military organizations share a secret. They have a discipline to discover their best options by answering this recurring question: What is the smallest step with the biggest return?

This book, with its stories and questions, intends to remind you to think about doing things in new ways. This is my book's one big idea: Find the smallest step with the biggest return. Then take it.

Marta Wilson
Arlington, VA
June 2012

EVA: COMMITTING TO EXCEPTIONAL CUSTOMER AWARENESS

The older I get, the greater power I seem to have to help the world; I am like a snowball—the further I am rolled, the more I gain. —Susan B. Anthony

Integrity is a cornerstone in successful lives and careers. Wherever you are and whatever you do, integrity has immediate value. It means that individuals can be trusted with critical responsibilities. You have good reason to entrust your enterprise to those working with you. Indeed, your business must become everybody's business.

This idea may seem idealistic, but it is quite serious. Current research into new business realities highlights new ways of working and a new kind of talent. I've culled that research for this book. We can speed to the end here: Scholars return again and again to the far greater potential that individuals hold in our new economy.

Transformation Systems, Inc. (TSI) is the company I launched in 2002 with a leap of faith and a credit card. Since then, the world in which I do business has evolved. TSI's vibrant teams of subject matter experts have been on the cutting edge of these new waves in modes of working. This book draws on extensive interviews with them. Their comments share a concern about the pressing need for innovation and continuous improvement. And they sound another, even more timely theme: Individuals can be innovators and leaders, no matter their job level or duties.

Let me start by explaining what I mean by "integrity." My colleagues and I work daily to renew the trust others place in us; chances are you do the same. With rare exceptions, so do most professionals. Such personal integrity becomes a building block for something larger, something that we have dubbed "enterprise integrity." As a professional team, we use personal integrity in our work restoring enterprise integrity for our clients.

Enterprise integrity involves correctly balancing all the moving pieces that make up an organization. Like the diverse instruments in a symphony orchestra, different factors in business—for example, goals, processes, talent, and outputs—can perform in concert for optimal results. Enterprise integrity characterizes a well-tuned business in which all the players are accurately performing the composer's score.

Also like an orchestral performance, enterprise integrity is not a static state. Organizations constantly shift, grow, contract, innovate, and otherwise respond to a tumultuous world.

Balance is not a set point but an art. It takes a lot of practice. The visionary leader is really a conductor.

My colleagues and I support leaders in particularly tough realignments that require radical breakthroughs. As with any good old-fashioned tune-up, in these realignments we see evidence that daily attention to needed organizational adjustments has suffered in the rush of activity. As we restore operational balance to the whole enterprise, we also design processes that empower individuals to act with unprecedented range. Thus, performance measures are about motivation, not restriction.

Most people associate large-scale organizational tune-ups with leadership, and I agree—to a point. As a leadership consultant who has for decades studied, supported, and provided professional development to executives, I have seen abundant evidence that impeccable leadership is critical for any organization to remain adaptable and viable. However, too much emphasis on a leader at the top lets far too many other people off the hook.

That's because every single person with some stake in an organization must be empowered to lead within his or her domain of responsibility. This person's leadership role may be fleeting and informal, or it may be official, complete with title and performance targets. Either way, no one is inconsequential in steering any enterprise to greatness, because greatness is achieved one decision, one action, and one person at a time.

Simply put, that's what *Everybody's Business* is about. How do you make it everybody's business to be sure that your organization achieves bold goals even in bleak times? And by everybody,

I mean not just employees but also customers, suppliers, strategic partners, and even competitors!

Let me save you from reading the last page and reveal the secret in the sauce: Everything depends on creating a culture where personal integrity can work in sync with enterprise integrity—the perfectly tuned, dynamic balance of discrete elements and participants—for all your stakeholders … every last one.

Consider Eva, my favorite waitress at my favorite restaurant, where I sometimes meet colleagues for business dinners. I know I can trust Eva for consistent and quiet service. It was the night when everything fell apart that my regard for Eva's work ethic was tested. That night might have been a turning point after which any loyal customer would have been hesitant to return. Instead, based on Eva's leadership and resourcefulness, it made a far more loyal customer out of me.

The rare night of a million small glitches does happen, even in a stellar restaurant. I understand that problems are part of good business. But, as I sat with my two guests, I observed over their shoulders quite a scene unfolding in the hallway and at the server stations. The bustle was chaotic: Servers were bumping into each other in the race to wait on their tables; unseated customers were huddled and watchful in full view; a suspicious smoke was frothing from the kitchen; a plate was overturned on the way to a table; another plate was broken on the kitchen floor. There were a variety of signs that this was turning into a night of food-service infamy.

Yet my dining room was notably unaffected. Eva was one of only a few servers, and she had picked up some large parties.

She was in constant motion but managed to exude calm. She checked each plate for each course before stepping into the dining room. More than a few times she returned to the kitchen for adjustments. She arrived at every table focused on the people there, and nowhere else. One of my guests commented on her easy efficiency; she knew where everything was and was able to maneuver through the chaos without a single incident.

I noticed that Eva, aside from her own tables, was also assisting with the workload of her neighboring server. Such largesse is unusual for servers, who can tend to be protective about tips. Yet Eva juggled her own tables, keeping them at ease through their meals, and also stepped out to help others. She was making it her business to preserve the signature atmosphere of the restaurant. It occurred to me that Eva was deriving a sense of personal accomplishment by doing so.

You likely agree that Eva embodies an ideal employee. You may even have some plan in place for fostering a working environment where someone like Eva can thrive. But that's not enough anymore. You need to know how to create leaders and innovators by drawing out every team member's potential—one person at a time. In other words, Eva, as a contributor to group success, is scalable. I've done this type of work all my career.

You may have your doubts, or you may believe there is just not sufficient payoff from investing in a cultural transformation in your workplace. Most likely, however, you have tried to find and keep top-notch staff—and failed too often. While salary is indeed a key indicator in companies with a stable talent base, so is culture—one that is built one person at a time.

As one of my guests at the restaurant that night pointed out, Eva was fluent in the working system behind the restaurant; that was how she succeeded in an economy of steps and choices. She offset shortfalls in the kitchen staff by anticipating what to check and fixing what was lacking. She was free to supplement efforts of other servers with time saved and confidence gained. In turn, Eva gained substantial personal satisfaction. If my tip was any indicator, she also saw direct benefit. The restaurant's stellar training also revealed its worth that evening—in systems that expedited the flawless dinner Eva managed to serve us despite mayhem in the background.

It's much the same for anyone working for you. The more individuals understand the total system, the more they can contribute beyond the narrow confines of a specific job description. The more the systems are devised to let them contribute, the more they will. The more incentives and opportunities to shine they have, the more they will shine. *Everybody's Business* is not, however, about one more good human capital management program. If it were, I would have no need to write the book.

Take a look at so-called virtual organizations. Each one is a case study in how total systems thinking is becoming part of collective consciousness in the workplace. In networked settings, each person still seeks a working concept of the full project and organization. Conversely, with a bricks-and-mortar building, people can rely on physical context for a sense of unity. Without the building (and commute), however, people still create a framework, a system, into which they fit. The workplace becomes a concept, not a building. The concept is a system, not a desk. Studies show that successful work for teams that are not co-located occurs with a keen, shared sense of context. In other words, in new work realities, individuals spontaneously develop the big-picture viewpoint that is normally limited to leaders. Thus the new workplace cultures are fostering leadership qualities as a collateral benefit.

How does this relate to you? Maybe you know you've settled for the constraint of cautious goals. Maybe you can sense a blind spot that hinders your full view of the organization's potential. Or maybe you can see that your organization is falling short for reasons that still baffle you. What is certain is that until you are in a position to set goals that are equally bold and achievable, you are faltering without a big-enough picture to guide you.

One problem with the big picture is the bewildering variety of business improvements, all of which are needed to adapt and compete, that are vying for attention. You are forced to face the reality that many will be shelved for want of resources. How do you prioritize? What do you trade off? Do you even have a reliable approach to prioritizing and choosing tradeoffs?

Here's the question you really want to ask yourself: Do you know how to identify the lowest-cost changes and strategic adjustments that will create the biggest payoffs for the greatest number of people? You can discover this pivotal alternative when you access, expand, unite, and put in motion the total system of individuals who are connected to your enterprise.

If anyone knows the cumulative impact of small, strategic choices it's the skipper of a sailboat. My husband, Bob, and I often sail on the Chesapeake. While in motion, we focus on myriad onboard details and all the natural elements at play around us. Sailing relies on simultaneous instinct and calculations.

I love sailing. When your feet leave land, it's a lot easier to gain perspective on where you've been and where you want to go. Sailing and business are alike that way: They both get you from Point A to Point B—from wherever you are to a goal or destination. They're both about motion.

A sailboat is made to create motion. Its design and all its features have evolved over centuries of seafaring according to an economy of motion. Similarly, to paraphrase Harvey Mackay, organizations are also designed for motion. Leaders need to stay in motion to survive. Organizations that *sustain* motion *thrive*.

As one small factor at sea shifts, we make an adjustment to restore balance and we keep moving. Do you want to know how to make the small adjustment that offsets a sea change for your enterprise? In your enterprise, unlike when sailing a boat, you can seek ideas from everybody in the organization. They are likely to know more than you about the details and even about the total system.

So, ask yourself: Am I looking to make strategic adjustments that will access, expand, unite, and put into motion the leadership and innovation potential residing in all the stakeholders connected to my enterprise? If you answer yes, you're reading the right book.

Everybody's Business is a review of the old art and the new science behind achieving bold goals, one person at a time.

ONE SMALL STEP: ADOPTING A TOTAL SYSTEMS PERSPECTIVE

Nothing in life is to be feared, it is only to be understood.
Now is the time to understand more, so that we may fear less.
—Marie Curie

When Neil Armstrong's foot dropped off the last step of the lunar module and onto the surface of the moon, he coined the famous phrase that his one small step was a giant leap for mankind. A single footstep had advanced human achievement. In the same way, any one person involved in your entire enterprise can move it forward exponentially. Identifying those individuals and choosing the right steps is what this book is about.

A whole team of unseen people stood behind Armstrong. Besides his family and friends, Armstrong relied on a close partnership with colleagues at NASA. That NASA A-team, in turn, was building on the expertise and achievements of many others who preceded them. Armstrong stood on the shoulders of giants long before he took his one small step. This book is about getting to the small steps in your organization—those instances that are, indeed, watershed moments of success—in the only way possible: by creating teams of giants. That's why this book, despite the economic climate in place as I write these words, is an optimistic assertion for envisioning bold goals and achieving unimaginable results, one person, one step at a time.

Around the world and close to home, our organizations have become more networked. Our macro and micro challenges are ever more complicated, and our technologies are constantly advancing. The expertise of each individual is even more critical for shared knowledge and the innovative exchange of ideas. One way of looking at it is that everybody is needed for collective success. Individual performance is everybody's concern.

Research over the past few years is starting to detail a working world that no one would have predicted in decades past. Our working relationships are radically different. We all know business teams are using teleconferencing to collaborate across the country and around the world. Yet, it would have been harder to predict that the shift to network technology would have such impact even where it's not strictly needed. For example, even if a colleague is located down the hall rather than across the continent, many people will communicate by sending an email or text message instead of visiting the individual's office or even making a phone call.

We are choosing to experience each other in radically new ways. Our collective work in particular conjures up our ability to imagine context. As work grows more networked (or, in some industries, more "virtual"), our creative bonds are adapting to technology. Or rather, technology is leaving its imprint on our teams and on us as individuals. This shift offers an important opportunity, a new juncture where businesses can choose to build success from the individual up.

For example, it was always true that any individual might need to lead a group effort occasionally. In a bricks-and-mortar setting, every individual still finds him- or herself called upon to lead from time to time. This is not the same as the more visible, formally assigned role of leader.

It is common for leadership to be informal and fleeting; people rise to meet the unexpected challenge and then resume business as usual. What defines the success of formal leaders is how well they empower everybody else to rise to the occasion. Are people around you ready and poised to apply their knowledge and abilities to forge a solution and achieve great things at a moment's notice?

Whether informal or formal, leadership styles vary; leadership visions vary. Even the degree to which any organization must change can vary. The constant, however, is that excellence is achieved, time and time again, by the leader who institutionalizes a culture of continuous improvement, a leader who can enable responsiveness and flexibility in an ever-changing market. Flexibility is the key to enterprise health, wealth, and creative power.

But a culture of continuous improvement relies on individual commitment. Like that one step onto the lunar surface, an enterprise requires individuals to achieve transformation.

Indeed, the truth is that you can't change an enterprise. What you can do is inspire individuals to commit to changing themselves and their work.

My own commitment to continuous improvement started early in my career. After receiving my PhD in industrial and organizational psychology, I was traveling around the country and internationally as an organizational transformation consultant. With every new engagement, I found myself learning how much the individuals involved already knew about the very solution that seemed to elude them. Now, as technology breaks down silos and hierarchy, the voices of knowledgeable participants that were silent then are far easier to hear—and to amplify.

For my part, I wanted to keep learning as a way to pursue avenues that would help these great companies unlock their own potential. Soon I was spending most of my free hours and disposable income in seminars, absorbing applied wisdom from prominent scholars and change gurus like W. Edwards Deming, Peter Senge, Deepak Chopra, Meg Wheatley, Stephen Covey, and Carol Pearson. These names are legendary; their works are classics in business. While different in style and viewpoint, they all approach organizations holistically.

The holistic approach to business is classic, and classics matter. Their impact is far-reaching. George Lucas credits Jules Verne with inspiring his creative achievements. Shakespeare still influences performances, even in sitcoms like *Third Rock from the Sun*, whose lead "alien" says he created his signature grandiosity from his Shakespearean training. And some even admit to reliving the joy of LEGO® bricks as they play SimCity.

Classics beget classics in literature and technology, and the same applies to business classics. Thought leaders who championed continuous improvement also believed in the power of one individual to launch large-scale change. They believed that one person's improved expertise could ensure the success trajectory of a whole group.

One person, one action has organization-wide value. This was true when the classic total systems thinkers were leading business into a new era of global competition, and it is truer now. The first step to unleashing the potential of individuals to improve your total organization is to get some concept of your enterprise as a working system, a total system. Various models exist to help portray an enterprise in this way. Indeed, many business models exist. They all tease out, in one way or another, distinct parts of the whole system, providing a starting point for how one change in one area can affect people and processes throughout the organization.

Over time in many industries, the SIPOC model has successfully guided assessment activities in full-throttle organizations. Its name is an acronym drawn from the elements it uses to define an organization: suppliers, inputs, processes, outputs, and customers. But SIPOC is not the only model. Different models are helpful in different ways. In light of the research in new working environments, it's interesting how total systems models emphasize a central role for people. SIPOC, for example, is largely about human beings. SIPOC and other models reflect how a total organization can improve when one person or group gets smarter, reaches a benchmark, or employs a bright innovation.

When you see how one person can have organizational impact and how one task can have enterprise-wide impact, you can start to turn the formula around. Whenever you face a large-scale problem, you can begin by looking for changes that will solve many problems (or seize many opportunities) across the whole organization. That's why it's important to remember the special value of the human element in total systems. The human level is where continuous improvement occurs in organizations. Your role as a leader is to draw on each person's fluency in one or two areas of a total system in order to improve the whole.

Consider suppliers: The SIPOC model gives them prominence. Their performance has profound impact on enterprise success. Their firsthand experience of your organization's work effectiveness can provide feedback that moves from the point of contact all the way to affecting choices in product design or directions in service expertise. Suppliers are particularly central as strategic partners—and sources of market information. These key partners can actually bring their expertise to bear and create solutions to support success, if you take the time to explain to them your business needs and goals. This is total systems thinking in action. Have you talked with and listened to your key suppliers lately?

Using the SIPOC model, customers are another great source

for ideas to improve your products or services. Do you have a sufficient dialogue in place to discover ideas from customers' unique vantage point? The same goes for your employees and contractors. Add to these the other stakeholders and people who interact with your organization in any way, from investors and media to the community-service groups with whom your staff may volunteer.

Each of these individuals has something to say worth hearing. They offer a comprehensive image of your total system at work. Here is where your quality of leadership is tested, even reworked. To begin, are you able to listen with an open mind to good and bad reviews? With a more updated approach, you also need to evaluate whether everybody in your business is listening, because everybody is asked to lead innovatively.

Listening is not the only quality needed in a culture of excellence. Leaders who are able to transform enterprises into rapidly responsive and adaptable groups tend to share similar qualities. Now everybody in the organization needs to foster the same attributes. These qualities, summarized below, have great impact on bottom-line success. How? Through the bonds they create among everyone involved in your business. By fostering these collaborative bonds, leaders have access to all the best each person has to offer.

In fact, this holds true for me personally and professionally. As the founder of a consulting company comprised of highly credentialed subject-matter experts, I have a particular interest in turning to my employees. They inspire me and each other. They innovate. They motivate. They value everyone's ideas and are able to take the long view. My colleagues at TSI are wonderful counsel.

These experts all agree that there are a few fundamental characteristics of successful leaders. They notice in the workplace what academic research points out: These qualities are desirable in all employees and in others who are in a position to help your business. These key attributes should no longer be reserved for official leaders.

Leadership Qualities for Everybody

Long-term View

Big Picture

Vision

Delegation

Motivation

Inclusivity

Self-awareness

Resourcefulness

Leaders take a *long-term view*. Certainly, from time to time they may set aside a grander view to complete a project on time and on budget. Largely, however, leaders balance schedule and quality with people's needs. They understand how retention and engagement serve the organization as well as its employees.

Leaders see the *big picture*. They grasp how actions by one can affect many others. They also inspire others to think beyond their current domain of responsibility and gain a working knowledge of the greater system in which they work. This way, leaders inspire the leadership mindset in others.

Leaders provide *vision* to unify people's energy and to inspire their actions. By being consistent, they also help align all work decisions. A clear vision permits people to act innovatively, because they have aligned their view and goals with the larger system.

Leaders *delegate*, but they don't stop there. They also provide support and necessary resources while avoiding micromanaging and abandonment. Among colleagues, the person with leadership qualities is supportive and encourages bold, reasoned choices and actions.

Leaders *motivate*; they rally emotional energy in teams. They motivate through personal connection and through sharing the image of a total system. They understand that emotional energy can be fueled by vision and clarity.

Leaders are *inclusive*. They engage diverse interests and activities by establishing goals and fostering a shared awareness. Here, their work is like that of the conductor of an orchestra, including an appreciation for the social aspect of a group endeavor. Like Eva in the restaurant, they have the operation of the whole in mind, even as they tend to the particular.

Leaders are *self-aware*. They have a keen sense of their greatest strengths and growth opportunities, and they continuously work for personal and professional improvement. Also, to increase their self-awareness, they consistently seek feedback from those around them.

Leaders are *resourceful*; they know their system. They are skilled at maneuvering around yet complying with policies and procedures. They don't give up until the right thing is done right.

These qualities in people who have some stake in your organization can lead to a surge in innovations and solutions—a lineup of expert support worth encouraging. As a first step, I suggest getting a grip on your total system and beginning to understand the unique human factor that is changing even the classical solutions for organizational growth and change.

In the next chapters, we'll move through some of the proven solutions leveraged today by successful executives. Along the way, I'll describe how sea changes in our world are affecting the strategies you need in your business for the years ahead—and what you can do to get on the right course and navigate the white water of change.

PIXELS: ASSESSING ORGANIZATIONAL PERFORMANCE

Everyone in a complex system has a slightly different interpretation. The more interpretations we gather, the easier it becomes to gain a sense of the whole. —Margaret J. Wheatley

L eaders these days can face continuous perplexity and anxiety as they try to get a handle on the big picture. Business and government must grapple with challenges that defy compromise or delay. Budgets are tightening. Meanwhile, technology, acquisition, and logistics advance and grow increasingly complex. The work done on one desk, whether commercial or government, can have instantaneous global impact. What this means is that the old marketing hype is no longer cliché: Companies that rely on yesterday's solutions will be weeded out, and others will take their place. We see it happening all around us.

Whether you're in business or government, you're likely under pressure to find new ways to sustain results with current resources. You may even need to increase profits or results without adding to current expense levels. Or, most likely, you've been told to do more with less. No one seems free anymore to sit back and rely on the status quo. You must adapt your enterprise to the big picture we all share. Where do you start, especially when you thought you were already adapting?

You've been working hard at adapting. It's likely you're already working to gather information to identify key priorities. You're probably involved in some kind of tactical planning for immediate circumstances. Many of you may be operating within a large-scale strategic plan.

Let's take a look at information gathering. You've assessed your organization, you say; you can't afford another assessment. The process can be disruptive of daily work. The only way to minimize the drag on people's work is by confining information gathering to a single exercise. Surely I can't be suggesting you repeat that kind of large-scale project? Yes, I'm suggesting a courageous organizational assessment.

Let's put it this way. Big answers to our perception of the big picture start at the pixel level. You need to get granular in your information collection. Think of the pixel, the smallest discrete element of a digital image. It's the tiniest "dot" inside a digital photo. Pixels vary in intensity depending on how many tiny elements get piled on top of each other. The more intense the pixel, the clearer the image will be.

Organizational assessments have promised snapshots of "current state." What you need these days are high-resolution real-time images. That's where the second purpose of an organizational assessment comes in to play.

The second and more important purpose of an organizational assessment is to kick off a dynamic exchange of ideas among all the parties who have anything to offer. It lets everybody contribute their pixels to be sure your image is as accurate as possible.

Every company needs this internal dialogue. It cannot be limited to a short-term assessment. Open, honest, and direct dialogue needs to be embedded in the culture. The constant dynamic interaction of ideas will sustain maximum accuracy. Your "current state" can adjust itself, pixel by pixel. With this internal interaction among all the best of your talented people, you have what it takes for great decisions. The first order of business is to establish this high-quality conversation with everybody in your enterprise.

To be clear, I'm saying that "current state" snapshots are not enough. You need living images that can adjust as needed on a granular level. Your decision making is daily; so should be your information gathering. You must foster fruitful conversations with everybody in your business. That includes dialogue with employees, strategic partners, vendors, and especially customers. This dialogue is how you ensure immediate access to a wealth of knowledge and experience to guide priorities, market responses, and innovations.

How to begin? Assess the situation. Many leaders think of an organizational assessment as a luxury, something that would be nice if only there were time. Or they mistake it for the above-mentioned one-time, disruptive, information-gathering diagnostic exercise. They're stuck focusing on getting information. That's not a good starting point for clearing the lens you use to see the business in the context of the big picture.

A robust organizational assessment must measure and portray all the pixels in a "current state" snapshot. That's not all. It must also be the first step in revitalizing an internal dialogue where everybody can be heard and where every viewpoint provides information on immediate issues and long-term success. An organizational assessment is about energizing everybody to participate in a free exchange of ideas. It kicks off a new level of thinking, dialogue, and creativity. It begins to remind people of old social skills in a new business setting. Other steps covered in later chapters keep the dialogue going, and the dialogue needs a good foundation. That foundation begins with the first image, the starting point.

This brings us to the idea of everybody being critical to business success. The organizational assessment finds and taps ideas from those people who have already encountered first-degree problems—and imagined ways to adjust—long before leadership has even recognized the crisis. These individuals are not often in a position to implement good ideas. Often, they don't have a voice in struggling organizations, whose trials and tribulations often reflect that they've stopped listening to the full range of people who understand any dilemma!

By contrast, consider what Hilton Worldwide has done. In its six-line values statement, it gives a prominent role to everyone in the business having "ownership" of decisions and the actions they create. "Hilton brands touch hundreds of communities and millions of people every day," Christopher Nassetta, president and chief executive officer of Hilton Worldwide is quoted as saying.[1] Do you empower everyone in your organization with that much responsibility? Do you trust them enough to do so?

If you don't, it's not for want of options. You have at your disposal right now people expert in your business. They are already working for you. They have ideas and experiences that can create a real-time info feed into your office for consideration with the same constancy of stock-quotes across an investor's screen. Why not? You're already investing in this talent. Every day can be payback for you, especially when your success has become everybody's business.

With a high-res picture of the whole, you'll be able to see how everybody has insights into making your business work better, leaner, faster, and smarter. Their experience and wisdom can be gathered and organized in a rigorous organizational assessment, and the need to keep that info feed energetically ongoing is critical. It's a fundamental element in a worthwhile organizational assessment. Especially in organizations that have gone through upheaval or acquisitions, the wisdom of the employees is often overlooked. The assessment must shine a bright light on their work and their smarts.

There you have it. This is my assertion for creating a well-informed baseline. You need the right kind of organizational assessment: One that helps set priorities; one that spurs choosing the right, effective action for immediate concerns and the long term; and, optimally, one that ignites an exchange of ideas. This is the fastest and most effective way to imbed knowledge-able dialogue in business routines to be sure quick changes can be made whenever needed.

So, if you are feeling at all unclear about a vexing problem, ask yourself whether you've checked the pixels in the image. Check for a real-time info feed in your enterprise. Listen for the banter of smart people—wherever they are located within your enterprise. These are some signals that you've done everything possible to enable yourself to rely on the power of the ideas in exchange around you in order to move the organization forward.

DIALOGUE AND INNOVATION

In *Leaders in Motion: Winning the Race for Organizational Health, Wealth and Creative Power*, I was reflecting on how leaders catalyze new ways of thinking in their organization when I wrote, "The effort to overcome inertia often pits leaders against their organizations—for a while."[2] There's no doubt people have a hard time changing habits of communication. That's another way an organizational assessment can help: It works around, not against, inertia with a formalized task of creating an accurate "current state," high-resolution snapshot.

Since I wrote that line in my book, my perspective on new thinking has evolved. Kicking up the dialogue to a whole new level is more critical than I previously believed! Such dialogue really is the heart of innovation on a scale that exceeds the lone genius or the dynamic duo just leaving grad school. It can be exactly where innovation occurs.

Prospective clients, especially, tell my teams that resistance is greater than ever to the chaos that new thinking in existing organizations can unleash. Often, these are the businesses most in need of innovation, but their people are already overwhelmed. Even the people with the best ideas may be too busy to notice they have anything to offer, unless you put their contribution in the context of what everybody else has to offer.

That's your work. You can benefit from the dynamic dialogue, and you can also drive it forward when everyone complains they have no time to think in new ways or to imagine big enough to confront the big picture. You must be in dialogue, because you must keep people engaged.

Addressing leading businesses in the Northern Virginia area recently, Wes Bush, chairman, CEO, and president of Northrop Grumman, gave a speech titled "Securing the Nation: An Industry Perspective" that was concerned with the utmost importance of innovation in our national defense and in our national economy as a whole. He reminded us that the exceptional leadership of our war fighters is drawn from an industry that has championed cutting-edge innovation. Bush also showcased the innovative energies of industry in its support of our national security. His vision is a total systems idea in which an industry serves each war fighter one breakthrough idea at a time.

When it comes to innovation, Bush takes a much-needed big-picture view of the more typical image most people have: an outdated image too limited to confront the daunting challenges of our day. Inspiration may dawn one idea at a time, but innovation is often a collective achievement that relies on everyone taking ownership of a shared cause.

Often, when asked about innovation, people imagine a lone genius. Their idea might run something like the experience of Ernie Fraze when he realized he had forgotten to bring a can opener to a picnic. Resorting to the car bumper to pry the soda cans open, he had within a month conjured up an alternative—the pop-top can. His invention solved his picnic problem, and within just twenty years his small but successful engineering company was raking in over $500 million dollars of annual revenue.[3]

Or there are entrepreneurial duos like Scott Jones, a researcher at MIT, and Greg Carr, a Harvard graduate student, who launched their own company to provide call-in stock quotes to subscribers. In the process, they inadvertently came up with voice mail, which was a staple of business until text messaging started to overtake its use in the past few years—but not before Jones and Carr became multimillionaires. From invention to market, the process took three months.[4]

These inspiring stories about individuals making it big are important for each of us, and at the same time Wes Bush's advocacy for industry innovation is important to us all. Imagine if Fraze or Jones and Carr were on your payroll. Indeed, they may be. Your enterprise needs solutions as much as partiers at picnics without can openers needed a solution and a population without voice mail needed a breakthrough. Do you know where all the innovators are in your organization?

Your enterprise also needs to be able to get from idea to implementation as fast as a couple of driven individuals. Do you know the impediments to that kind of speed and the strengths needed to achieve the fastest response time for you? The good news is that your company or agency can back the innovators and take their work to the next step.

You alone cannot know the answer to any of these questions. You need the benefit of a dynamic dialogue among people inside and outside your organization. That's what brings your working ideas into real time. That's what you need to respond to serendipity.

It's old thinking to limit innovation to the lone genius or to the enterprising duos. Innovation is underway already in your business and in our economy. As Wes Bush said to the hundreds of business leaders listening to him, fostering innovation has never been more important for your business, our economy, or our national security.

Ikujiro Nonaka agrees. This great author co-wrote *The Knowledge-Creating Company* with Hirotaka Takeuchi and was listed by the *Wall Street Journal* in 2008 as one of the most influential persons on business thinking. Nonaka makes no bones about it: He links business success to an ability to create knowledge, to innovate, by "tapping the tacit and often highly subjective insights, intuitions, and hunches of individual employees and making those insights available for testing and use by the company as a whole."[5]

The dynamic dialogue we help our clients foster is what captures all these insights, intuitions, and hunches, along with all the research, empirical data, and experience of everybody involved. This is the exchange of ideas that makes everybody smarter—employees, suppliers, and customers alike. This is the dialogue an artful organizational assessment kicks off. Such dialogue keeps valued people in-house and critical suppliers and customers coming back.

The alternative to this creative exchange of ideas is troubling: Your best talent becomes disenfranchised; your customers and other strategic partners drift away; the innovation and change they might have inspired is lost. The impact can extend beyond your bottom line and upturn an industry. Remember: Where an outdated model cannot adapt into a timely one, it will be replaced by something else.

That's the story of the emergence of Silicon Valley. Eight dissatisfied employees of Shockley Semiconductor left en masse to form an independent firm, Fairchild Semiconductor, only to leave again to start their own companies. Innovators continued to hatch out of the subsequent businesses to seize new opportunities. That's how we all came to see that, in just twenty years, sixty-five new businesses came into being where in 1957 there had been only Shockley Semiconductor. While we all applaud Silicon Valley and its great impact on the industry, its emergence is also an allegory—and perhaps a cautionary tale—for finding ways to make established organizations places where innovators can remain, enfranchised and thriving. You could say the moral of the story is you can rely on serendipity only as long as you don't rely on serendipity alone. For that, you need some organized way for the disorder of a dynamic dialogue to have innovative impact every day.

CHAT WITH AN EXPERT: DR. WILLIAM BRACKEN

Bill Bracken was recently sharing how several leaders he knew had a huge effect on the dynamic dialogue where they were working. The moral of the story is that leaders who want to keep the dialogue going need to adapt not just to circumstances but also to the people they rely on. I couldn't help thinking of how his allegory refers to leadership as being individualized, so that each person's unique talent is magnified for the sake of the total outcome.

Bill recounted how he once worked with a leader whose approach was abusive. "He was probably the smartest multidisciplinary person I've ever met. He was really quite a genius. But he also had some of the poorest people skills." Bill explained how the leader fired people regularly, explaining that, "I believe when I fire people, I'm doing them a favor. I'm giving them a wake-up call." Ultimately, this fellow found his niche by specializing in quick-turnaround ventures, where the skill in fostering long-term relationships with talented people didn't matter.

Bill noted how this leader's impact was usually astounding but seldom lasting, even where "there was an extreme emphasis on financial controls, because ultimately the people whose know-how the company needed to establish a strategy for sustained growth were either silenced or gone by the time the fellow had moved on. For a while, the company could afford to act like people were expendable; but even with a large pool of candidates they ultimately had a hard time restoring team productivity in his wake."

"The issue I see is that people prefer to stick to functional silos and lack the ability to create connections where seemingly none exist. People can't come to these realizations independently. They seldom change without situational challenges to create the momentum for dialogue and a group effort. Then they need an inclusive process that permits them to learn the skills for contributing freely where there are complex situations, complicated priorities, and dissenting views. This goes back to education in elementary school. Simplistic answers are not the right answers." —Bill Bracken

"People often have a negative opinion of autocratic leadership like this," Bill added, "but not all effective leadership is supportive or collegial. The best leadership is situational. It adapts. When time is of the essence or lives are at stake, there is not time to collaborate or engage people in consensus. Think of the *Titanic*."

Leaders who adapt to people are able to give individuals a great deal of freedom to contribute their best on their own terms. Unlike the turnaround expert with no people skills, leaders who adapt to people sustain results. As Bill recalled, "One manager I worked with was good with varying his leadership style based on the situation. If the individual lacked skill, he wouldn't delegate the assignment to her and instead used a more descriptive, detailed approach. If the individual had skills, he'd tell her the problem and let her take care of it. This involves a process of empowerment. Many managers make mistakes with empowerment. It doesn't mean abandonment; it means adjusting to each person's strengths and setting each individual on the course for success: from start to finish, being available in a way that helps and does not hinder. For different people, that may mean different things. Even if you empower a person or group, it requires follow-up and monitoring without being intrusive."

ASK YOURSELF

Are you on the fence about assessing the current state of your organization? If so, here are some questions for strategic reflection:

1. Do I have a confident sense of what my organization is committed to and how we are performing in the following areas: strategic planning, decision making, value streams, information technology, product line management, process improvement, human capital strategy, workforce development, and performance measurement?

2. Is my organization effectively gathering the information we need to identify key priorities and create tactical plans for a relentlessly changing world?

3. What priorities should we tackle first?

4. What are the barriers to getting things done more quickly?

5. What are our current indicators of how the organization is performing?

6. Do we have a consistent record of past performance for the total system?

7. How are different components (suppliers, inputs, processes, outputs, and customers) linked together?

NEXUS: PLANNING STRATEGICALLY
TO PROPEL FORWARD

And no, we don't know where it will lead. We just know there's something much bigger than any of us here. —Steve Jobs

"**N**exus" is a fun word, especially in our world today. It has a special meaning for all of us because it is, after all, the new name used to replace "World Wide Web" when people want to avoid confusion between the web browser that shared the same name as the infinite world it was searching. "Nexus" is also a word that will soon be an international standard for data being shared by scientists around the globe who are trying to talk about neutrons and X rays. Nexus gets around, and it's always hard at work relating connections. Nexus surfs the World Wide Web, finding significant points we seek, and it permits scientists and programmers to speak the same language. Nexus is a central point in a fluid web. Indeed, in many cases, nexus is the intersection of forces requiring a decision that affects everything that follows.

Nexus, for business, rests in the power of decisions to create each step forward. How are you sure you're moving forward in the right direction? Where's the compass? Where's the plan?

One great misconception about strategic planning is that it sets in stone a course for the long haul. For those of us in the business of nimble, responsive strategic plans, the very idea seems linear, stale before it's done—rote. I'm thinking of a word, and that word is "boring."

By contrast, in our work we know how a strategic plan can create impeccable decision makers. That's because a successful plan puts everybody at work in the same place. In other words, a plan creates nexus. Everyone's work is connected by common understandings, and day by day, everybody shares the vital nexus, here and now. All the right people have all the right information to make all the best decisions that move everybody forward—one person, one decision at a time.

A strategic plan isn't so much a piece of paper as a shift in mind. It moves responsibility for a company out of the hands of a few executives and into the hands—and heads—of everybody working the plan. For success, a strategic plan is a daily awareness. It's simple. A strategic plan is what makes sure that the vessel leaves the hands of the manufacturer and is handed over to crew for passage to bolder destinations. Each person relies on his or her own power for many key decisions and knows when to turn to leadership for guidance with larger, collective changes.

In favorable circumstances, it's not counterintuitive to surrender a great enterprise to an enterprising crew. However, difficult times can tempt the best leaders to grip control more tightly. The times are urgent, after all, right? We can't afford to miss any opportunity to reduce, advance, create, surpass, or preserve in this complicated and global economy. Shouldn't leadership be more hands-on?

Hold it right there. A strategic plan is the best way—whether sailing is smooth or rough—for you to be involved in every decision without being in the way. The plan is a robust guide that keeps you from exerting a dampening influence on your teams. When you step out using a strategic plan, you can count on unleashing the full power of your organization's talent. Once a strategy is planned and in place, your only remaining challenge is stepping back, listening, and being humbled by the brilliance you find working for you.

That's because a strategic plan can and must be the single most important step that imbeds creative dialogue and the exchange of ideas in a business culture. In this dynamic, you participate but don't risk dominating. The plan helps you leverage the best people, the brightest ideas, and all the energy they generate to drive everybody forward.

How is this done? The well-crafted strategic plan isn't complicated, although its development can take some time. The goal is clarity, and the process is energizing. What you have, in the end, is a shared understanding that becomes a familiar reference point. It's used as a surefire way for each person to move forward independently without creating chaos or downward drag. This plan becomes the filter for sifting out meaning from all the noise among the rush of daily priorities.

A strategic plan doesn't start on a blank sheet of paper. It builds on the organizational assessment that precedes it. The high-res info feed now becomes integral to how the business works and shares information—and also for the quality of information you have for keeping executive-level decisions in tune with what your people are doing. It also removes impediments to decision making, because everybody knows the parameters for choices and the end goal that drives them.

Rapid response is possible no matter how large or far-flung your enterprise, and strategic planning is the key to rapid response, empowering everybody working ably within their spheres to be poised to make decisions quickly and in synch with everybody else.

We know that threats abound for our military—and for global commerce. Fast-changing opportunities to advance and succeed require rapid response rates possible only when decisions are made with alignment of purpose and work is performed across divisions. Despite what anyone may claim, any large organization can turn on a dime—if all its pieces are aligned and working in unison when the decision point arrives. I know. I have seen this happen again and again, as organizations that are stalled or sluggish energize their full forces by aligning processes and people with a crystal-clear plan.

The very word "alignment" is a clue that enterprise integrity is the issue. In other words, enterprise integrity ensures rapid response. And I know from experience that enterprise integrity relies on a solid strategic plan.

Think of it this way. Enterprise integrity is about balancing all the moving pieces that make up an organization. Like diverse instruments in a fine orchestra, different factors—for example, goals, processes, talent, and outputs—are made to work in concert for optimal results. Enterprise integrity is a well-tuned business following an expertly composed score.

Enterprise integrity is not a static state. Organizations constantly shift, grow, contract, innovate, and otherwise respond to a tumultuous world. Balance is not a set point but an art. It takes a lot of practice. As stated earlier, the leader is, in the best of circumstances, a conductor.

Sure, this sounds great, but we've all been in offices where "harmony" is hardly the right descriptor. That's because there is no single, real, active plan unifying people and work goals. All too often, though there is a plan, one no one takes it seriously as it sits in a three-ring notebook on an executive's shelf. Having watched, over the years, the impact of a well-honed strategic plan on a business endeavor, I find it a shame that people slog to work to be part audience, part player in a poorly tuned, cacophonous symphony. It doesn't matter if there is a skilled conductor—or executive—if there's no sheet music from which to play.

Just like an orchestra with its various instrumental sections, there are various subgroups within your enterprise. It's natural for subsystems habitually to act independently and, all too often, at cross-purposes. But strategic plans are the integrating factor. They carry your leadership to the level of the individual instrument. They drill down into roles and responsibilities—and performance measures. Execution becomes smooth. There is little waste of effort and little reason for decision-making angst. Your team is finally working in unison, empowered to implement the daring decisions needed for triumph.

Only with strategic planning can you get the musical score squared away so that you, as conductor, can restore order—enterprise integrity—among all the various parts of the ensemble.

If you want to be ready not only to respond to serendipity but also to foster it, the strategic plan is a way to organize the disorder of a dynamic dialogue so that it can have innovative impact every day. The plan creates the unity that can seize upon the unexpected to achieve the unimagined.

That's because plans institutionalize the very routines that foster a comfortable and continuous exchange of ideas and creative dialogue. Quite counter to the usual bias about planning, effective strategic plans magnify creativity and action.

So, maybe it's time to expand your own view of the power of a strategic plan. Let everyone in your organization know where you are headed, how they can help, and what success looks like at the end of the journey. From inception through completion and implementation, strategic planning is really about one thing, and that is not a three-inch, three-ring notebook with pretty tabs. It's about the creative dialogue and exchange of ideas you need to keep that high-res info feed running through your office and your business to keep processes constantly improving, decisions regularly spot-on, and people motivated to whole new levels of participation within a vibrant work culture. How? Everybody becomes as versed in the business as you are. Each person gets to own the whole success of the enterprise.

Just to be really clear, it's critical that strategic planning kicks off a new level of conversation and then, during implementation, fosters and generates dialogue daily. That dialogue becomes the guide for future decisions. That empowerment to judge and decide is what the plan establishes. The dialogue vests a lot of power in everybody who participates.

Great strategic planning isn't just a plan. As a plan, it doesn't overshadow the living, daily pulse of business. Strategic planning, from start to implementation, is a continuing conversation about what people in the organization want to create, the culture they envision, and the business results they need. Your powerful combination of intention and mechanism sparks imagination that ignites bold goals and passion for positive action. It forges a clear decision path that brings unity to cross-purposes and confidence to hesitation. As a result, talent is focused on achieving shared success and resources are used for incremental growth—not status quo.

DIALOGUE AND CLARITY

In the 1960s Igor Ansoff wrote the seminal book *Corporate Strategy*. Like many watershed business books, Ansoff's captured the times, when strategic planning as a discipline was fresh and being received with widespread enthusiasm in businesses of all levels. You may best know Ansoff as the creator of the idea of business "synergy" and the iconic formula 2+2=5. Within thirty years, however, the grand idea was being criticized. One management rebel, of sorts, named Henry Mintzberg, wrote *The Rise and Fall of Strategic Planning*,[6] which critics robustly dismissed as portraying strategic planning as an empty ritual without adding value. Yet Mintzberg had some pretty undeniable data: The US Planning Forum had calculated that only 25 percent of companies rated their planning as effective.

It's true I founded and lead a company that uses strategic planning to enrich all aspects of business activities, and yet I still agree with Mintzberg's critique of strategic planning. In particular, his criticism contained the shining gem of the work of my colleagues. Mintzberg admitted that strategic planners can be effective when they unearth strategies already at work in pockets of the organization. That's when planning is most effective— when we unlock the value and power of what is undiscovered and untapped in any organization. We do that through rejecting the idea of an empty ritual in planning and determinedly fostering a creative dialogue and exchange of ideas that alone can create the clarity to empower everybody to own their piece of the business and to thrive.

Tapping creative dialogue for clarity, the CEO of Molson Coors Brewing Company, Peter Swinburn, turned around a situation in 2008 that bears a striking resemblance to what many of us face today. Various subgroups within the newly merged Molson Coors, in a joint venture with Miller, were operating with distinct cultures and at cross-purposes left over from past endeavors. Yet, the company had set the audacious goal of "achieving recognition as one of the world's top brewers in a fiercely competitive global beer market." Swinburn knew that, given the resources and competition, all employees would need to pull together.

Swinburn kicked up the dialogue. He tasked a "team of clue hunters" with interviewing hundreds of employees about their likes and dislikes regarding the company culture and with reporting results back to the executive team. The "Our Brew" objectives grew out of this movement. These included Molson Coors committing to engaging employees, taking corporate responsibility, and monitoring progress. "We are very focused on making sure that we have the right quality and caliber of people," Swinburn said during an interview,[7] "and also that they have a very clear view of what their role is in the organization." Swinburn credited the outcome of this clarity to be an employee-devised "One Brew": "When you have engaged employees, they will be willing to go above and beyond their job descriptions to help the company achieve its biggest ambition."[8] Through the active dialogue Swinburn launched, empowering employees with creative thinking and full participation, Molson Coors has positioned itself as a "major global player in the international beer industry."[9]

Now, you may wonder whether these leaders were involved in planning or managing people. The two are one and the same. In an economic era where the market is knowledge-based and all about innovating to be competitive, your people are not just employees—they are your capital. And that's how the contemporary strategic plan generates inspiration, energy, and empowerment exactly where you need it—while everybody's clear on what to do and where they're headed.

"Clarity affords focus," said Thomas J. Leonard, who's considered one of the twentieth century's leaders in personal coaching, an art he viewed as a highly evolved form of relating. Certainly an innovator, Leonard took that artful capacity for relating online. Among the first to grasp the power of distance-learning relationships, even in training for work as fundamentally interactive as coaching, Leonard launched a virtual university, TeleClass.com, in 1998. It has over 20,000 students, offering hundreds of virtual classes. So, make no mistake: No matter whether you are fostering creative dialogue in a small group that works just beyond the frame of your door in a brick-and-mortar building or with a diversified team scattered across the globe and interacting by teleconference, creative dialogue is possible and equally essential.

Every creative dialogue welcomes complications and even conflict in its progress toward clarity. Make sure you have grounded what everybody is saying and doing now in what everybody understands and has accepted as a shared strategic plan. In other words, if you want a creative dialogue to energize everything your business does, create a nexus where everybody is able to be their best, to do great things, and to have meaningful success in concert with each other.

CHAT WITH AN EXPERT: DR. ALTYN CLARK

Altyn Clark is the model PhD and possibility thinker. Humble, exceptionally thoughtful, and formidably intelligent, Altyn is a great foil for testing ideas and is the perfect person to ask about resistance to strategic planning. He told me, "Marta, it's all about the dialogue leaders either do or don't want to have. At its best, strategic planning is an ongoing organizational conversation about people's activities and accomplishments. Discussing accountability for actions and results may feel risky, even to the most confident leaders, so they resist it.

"Results orientation is more critical than ever," Altyn told me, "and the pressure for immediate results amplifies the distrust many people have for the strategic planning process. Their experience has almost always involved a time-consuming exercise in futility that takes them away from their real work—and fails to add clarity in the end. Many times planning has been such a turn-off that people just endure the meetings so they can get back to their desks and work as soon as possible. I have been fortunate to work with many leaders over the years who see value in a crisp planning and review process that emphasizes execution for results. Their appreciation for a concise and focused plan may have spoiled me, I suppose. I am just accustomed to seeing results and kicking up results on a regular basis."

Altyn considers it a high honor to be working within the defense and national security community, especially because "I get to serve the people who serve the nation. My clients reflect the best of leadership, setting directions for subordinates and getting out of the way. These leaders manage to create space, even under fire, where people feel both free to and compelled to tax their own abilities, experience, and training to figure out the best way forward. They're permitted to have purpose, and once they make a choice with strategic implications, they stick to it. They find empowerment—rather than fear—in accountability.

"What I notice is the way the best of these leaders hold people accountable. It's all about a respectful, open dialogue," continued Altyn. "The leaders who avoid hard conversations are ineffective. There's no middle ground. Effective leaders know how to keep a great dialogue going—the good with the bad—and that's why they have no problem delegating. It's easier to take the risk to delegate when everybody knows—both leaders and team members—that the dialogue doesn't end with the assignment.

"Managing the ongoing dialogue isn't always easy." Is that the main reason plans fail to work for the people who make them? "Well, no. One thing we face is how promotions go to technically excellent people who often have no idea how to lead. They have the best intentions, but it proves a stumbling block when they need to mix more savvy interaction into their technical work. It's a nexus point. Either they acknowledge a need for their own growth and accept that it's possible to develop skills as a dialogue catalyst, or they don't.

"One of the single most daunting steps for a developing leader is to learn how to solicit feedback, listen to it, leverage it, replay it, and even encourage the respectful conflict it sometimes requires. Seeking feedback can feel extremely risky—so many people avoid it."

"First Things First: It's every leader's mandate to be accessible, and being accessible is the most difficult thing to do! The discipline pays off, because accessibility and approachability have everything to do with keeping the group moving forward and talking with ease and that's the number one way to achieve results." —Altyn Clark

Altyn believes "that's the billion-dollar question: How do we develop the willingness and even vulnerability required for these kinds of conversations? Without that level of personal authenticity it's hard for a leader to gain people's trust. With it, a leader can model for a group how to engage in a long-term dialogue about the strategic course and be sure great ideas and valuable answers will arise from active listening. Leaders use their plan like a guideline to keep the entire process moving forward.

"This capacity for strategic dialogue travels up as well as down the proverbial ladder," Altyn said. "Leaders forget that feedback is only part of the mix. They're in place to enhance the best in everybody, sometimes simply as an on-site coach with a keen sense of what people need to do and what they are capable of contributing. For the sake of their own people, leaders need to be willing to speak truth to power. To do that, they need to see and think at least one or two systems bigger than their current domain of responsibility. And to do that well, they need their own people doing the same thing. The best academic leaders are not thinking about their tenured position or department but about how to make their institution better or more effective overall. An effective supervisor in a Navy organization is not focused only on his or her domain but on how to contribute two or three levels up, at the PEO or command level."

Which brings us back to the total systems thinking, and to Eva, who knew how the full system around her worked and knew it well enough to deliver impeccable service and to make sure someone—namely she—was willing to assume responsibility for bolstering up the inevitable shortfalls in others' work. Eva didn't do this because of the strategic plan but because she found herself at a nexus when a well-planned setting permitted her to make rapid decisions that saved the day, or that saved my night, to be exact.

To use our other metaphor, such thinking typifies a skillful orchestral conductor who, amid the dynamic, ongoing flow of the music, can sense when the woodwinds are too soft, or the brass section too loud, and can guide the delicate adjustments that put the performance back into balance.

When anyone in your group finds himself at that kind of nexus, there's one way for you to be sure he can act with full ownership of the well-being of the organization: make sure he is fluent in the strategic plan and full force of the creative dialogue.

Remember to keep everybody at the nexus—fully informed and informing decisions fully.

ASK YOURSELF

Are you wavering about the relevance and importance of having a strategic plan? If so, here are some questions to guide your thinking:

1. Does everyone in my organization know where we are headed, how they can help, and what success looks like?

2. Does our planning approach involve the extended system, including customers, suppliers, and folks who represent a cross-section of employees?

3. What results and experiences do we want for our organization, and what are we willing to think, say, and do to create these results?

4. How will we know if we are achieving what we want?

5. Is a broad-scale decision badly needed in my organization that, for now, remains stalled in a floundering status quo?

6. What are the right criteria for choosing sound action?

7. How do we unify key leaders' divergent views?

5

ONE: DEVELOPING THE WORKFORCE INDIVIDUALLY

And I'd say one of the great lessons I've learned over the past couple of decades, from a management perspective, is that really, when you come down to it, it really is all about people and all about leadership. —Steve Case

The Samuel J. Heyman Service to America Medal is considered the most prestigious award bestowed on America's civil servants who are making high-impact contributions to the health, safety, and well-being of Americans. As the leader in a company dedicated to supporting the achievements of public servants, I'm always delighted to talk about the remarkable work that federal employees do every day, especially during an era when the largely dedicated federal workforce is generally underappreciated.

Service to America Medal winners personify what happens when one person commits with passion to a greater goal, leading others to greatness. Take Pius Bannis, field office director in Haiti for the US Citizenship and Immigration Services. In 2010 he was recognized with the Service to America Medal for expediting the immigration process to quickly unite more than 1,100 Haitian orphans with their adoptive families in the United States, following the devastating earthquake in January 2010. In 2009, Janet Kemp, the national director of the Suicide Prevention Program for the Department of Veteran Affairs was similarly recognized for establishing a national suicide prevention hotline for veterans that has resulted in more than 3,000 immediate rescues. In 2008, Richard Greene, director of the Office of Health, Infectious Diseases, and Nutrition of the US Agency for International Development, received the medal for designing and launching the President's Malaria Initiative, which has provided potentially life-saving services to more than twenty-five million vulnerable people.

These remarkable people used their leadership positions to take great leaps forward for the sake of country and individuals. Closer to home, other leaders do the same. For example, every year, the leading District business paper, the *Washington Business Journal*, announces awards for Women Who Mean Business. The awards recognize women from every industry and profession in the Metro DC area who've made a difference in their communities, leaving a unique mark as established leaders with a strong record of innovation in their fields, outstanding performance in their businesses, and meaningful community involvement.

A few years ago I was surprised by being recognized for "Meaning Business." The greatest aspect of the compliment was the lineup of other women business leaders and what they had achieved. Joining me on the stage were remarkable leaders such as Linda Cureton, chief information officer for NASA, and Linda Hudson, president of the land and armaments division of BAE Systems. Our actual work varied quite broadly, but as I was watching the award recipients speak in video clips, I was struck by a Margaret Mead line reminding that we should each "always remember you are absolutely unique, just like everyone else."

That brings to mind Suezette Steinhardt,[10] a fellow Virginia resident who doesn't seem unique like everybody else. By owning the need to help others solve otherwise daunting problems, Steinhardt was recognized by CNN as one of its heroes. Steinhardt, a suburban mom, created Family Preservation and Strengthening Services, or Family PASS, to help provide affordable housing and support services to low-income families. Her goal is to keep families out of shelters and on a path to self-sufficiency. "When we have an economy like this, the people at the very bottom are really going to be hit," said Steinhardt. "As a mother, as a neighbor to these families, I have to be a part of the solution of what's going on in our community." For Steinhardt, the key is bridging the gap between the time when families exit transitional housing programs and when they obtain affordable, permanent housing. Most of the clients in Steinhardt's program are single mothers struggling to make ends meet. "My mom was a single mom. She had four children. She started at minimum wage," she said. "I understand how hard it is for someone to raise a family in those circumstances." Steinhardt's mission began in 2004 after witnessing a single mother go through an ordeal trying to make it on her own. Steinhardt and her husband helped renegotiate the woman's lease, worked out a reasonable budget, and then made up the difference between her income and her budgeted needs.

The dreams and passions that inspire and drive us often become our signature contributions. Everybody can contribute their signature to their workplace or their community—if given a chance to express the ownership they feel. Think about it. Steinhardt's passion is quite remarkable, yet not so rare that you don't have people in your organization right now able to take ownership of some opportunity and, singularly, seize it with passion. You are looking for the Steinhardt quality to take a lead role in the community that is your business. No matter how far afield your team may be, it still is comprised of individuals, each of whom has the potential for some unique impact which only that individual can make.

There's power in one person, so be sure that everybody can be poised to make a difference when there's a difference to be made. Rededicate your own talent to creating a setting where everybody is rewarded for learning, collaborating, and succeeding. That's your very own power of one. There's a nexus coming. It's not necessarily you who will make the decision with impact. You don't know for sure whose turn it will be to take the wheel at a critical moment. That gives you a keen interest in making sure everybody is ready, because everybody's business is at stake.

Every individual can be in tune with your enterprise goals if you include them in the dialogue. Let me underscore "include."

Don't limit your idea of high-value contributors to employees. Look beyond the barriers of payroll to your customers, suppliers, strategic partners, and investors, to name a few. Each stakeholder has a unique take on what your organization is doing. Each one is a potential wealth of information for the real-time info feed that drives your creative dialogue forward into success.

Certainly, employees are most vested in success, and they are often the ones with an up-close experience of the dilemmas. Ideally, they're motivated to remove the burr from under the saddle faster than most other stakeholders. Seeking the right employees to yield this kind of influence becomes the highest goal. You're deciding not only the knowledge capital that will uphold the quality of what you provide to customers but also who will be problem solvers and innovators close to home.

Recently, my company advertised for a few open positions. The influx of volume was staggering, but fewer than a dozen represented professionals whose unique mix of training and experience seemed remotely close to our bottom-line criteria. This is the new hiring dilemma—great jobs, great people, poor match.

A good hiring process will identify a good hire, usually. Yet, think of the dilemma of a highly qualified person who is hired into the dynamic dialogue I'm encouraging you to supercharge in your organization. From the first day, the new employee will encounter positive conflicts more often than consensus as ideas are freely exchanged. There will be a fair amount of feedback with a high degree of accountability. Everybody will be vested in the new hire's success, which means everybody will be offering support, new information, and, quite possibly, surprising feedback.

There's nothing quite so disorienting for new employees as finding they are boarding a well-organized machine that is barreling forward like a high-speed train sure of its destination. So, yes, in the ideal setting, there will definitely be need for a rigorous orientation for new hires on how to contribute to everybody's business without getting lost or overcompensating by dominating. It is an outstanding accomplishment when you have achieved a cultural dialogue that creates this much challenge for every new hire.

The critical lesson to be learned about the power of one in your teams is in line with the rallying cry of today's business model. Most people are trying to do more with less. That forces them to first look more closely at what resources they already have. The same goes for talent. You're connected in your office or by virtual technology to a network of remarkable people whose potential I'm guessing you've hardly tapped.

Here's the great news. You don't need to recruit these people or invest time interviewing or on-boarding them. They already know about your business. The only obstacle to their being your next best lineup of opportunity is that a few may have succumbed to the effects of counterproductive attitudes—either their own or others. Here's the tough challenge. You need to see each individual with new eyes, both in terms of real value-add and in terms of future potential.

That said, take a look at your strategic plan. You already have people who, by now, have contributed in some way. They're already invested in the enterprise's success because, ideally, they've been consulted from the outset when the first assessment of the organization was made. They've participated in the discussion that led to a working strategic plan. Alternatively, maybe they've worked on one of the revitalizing initiatives reserved for the strategic plan that seems to be going nowhere, or that has gone awry. What's important is that individuals and groups are full participants. The assessment and the planning have been developmental opportunities. That is, you've learned from each other while taking the organizational dialogue up a few notches. Everybody is starting to mind the business.

But even with a positive culture forming, the realities remain harsh. Reduced budgets and an uncertain economy have placed ever-greater demands on each individual's output. Burnout tends to eclipse enthusiasm. Self-protective apathy saps commitment. Fear undermines focus, and conflicts unresolved in the crush of activity take lasting tolls on achievement. Turnover drains resources and disrupts work. Hiring and on-boarding are expensive—and risky. What is the cost of one poor decision? Of one unresolved conflict? Of one weak relationship? Of one disengaged leader?

Facing the realities will tend to bring us right back to the dynamic dialogue, with all its contradictions and bright energy. You must rely on strong and open discussion with everybody who has a role in your enterprise to take the pulse of the current state of the total system. The dialogue starts at the plan, and it also brings the plan along. With a clear strategic plan in place, roles will be clearer. Priorities will be easier to sort out. And you, above all, will be able to match task, project, and role to strengths.

By turning the organization into everybody's chance to strut their best stuff, you're able to trust in people confidently. You've made the culture into one where individuals shine in a way that advances the enterprise. This is alignment. This is another angle on enterprise integrity. This is the way to create a smoothly operating crew in full command of the ship's direction, an orchestra that plays in tempo and in tune.

I've heard it before: "These scenarios sound idealistic." Yes they do. Yet we know what our clients have done to create success. Either it's everybody's business, or it's a race lost. The competition is fierce for business and government alike. It's most obvious for our military. There is one goal in this competition, and that's to win. To win the race for enterprise excellence, you can't afford the drag on success that disorder and cacophony bring.

Competition is about teams and individuals. Both start with and rely on talent, and here, now, in our economy and in our global market, talent is central to flagship outcomes in an idea-driven world.

Experience and creativity are at the heart of success, especially in forging vibrant relationships and the innovation they drive. It's not enough to achieve a goal or to have a great idea. It takes energetic, committed talent to sustain success after the first hurdle is cleared. To support the development of key contributors, you have a huge range of tools to assess skills, potential, and problems in groups and individuals. Do you want your enterprise to be prepared to turn on a dime? Then develop your workforce one at a time, with the meticulous attention of any master at any craft. In the end, you have many tools at your disposal for motivating people. Performance measures grounded in a clear, strategic plan make for professional growth aligned with enterprise success, because they align individual with organizational goals. It's the best way for you to put individuals and groups in charge of the enterprise whose future is their future.

A big variable is you as a leader. You have the Power of One here, too. You need to be resourceful to engage your people with fresh eyes, build on their unique strengths, offset their individual weaknesses, and fashion a full course of action to move the organization forward by improving "one person at a time."

I'm reminded of the Robert Heinlein quote "When one teaches, two learn." The more you come to terms with the Power of One in your domain of influence, the more the people involved in the creative dialogue will be able to teach you in return.

DIALOGUE AND PEOPLE

By now, it's classic management history. Running from 1927 to 1932, the Hawthorne Studies at Western Electric's Chicago plant made a watershed link between workforce morale and organizational performance that radically changed management theory. One of the researchers, Elton Mayo, recorded the studies in a cornerstone book titled *The Human Problems of an Industrial Civilization*. Particularly surprising was the finding that individuals who have a sense of belonging to a group exhibit greatly improved performance. Individuals performed better individually if they were part of something greater. In today's terms, it's a truth seen in virtual companies where team members sit at desks in different locations than their team-mates; their success relies on the dialogue provided by new-tech communication options. The result is still greater than the individual parts, or, as Ansoff put it some years after Mayo, indeed, 2+2=5.

Douglas McGregor, in yet another flagship work titled *The Human Side of Enterprise*, marked the end of a traditional management approach, which he famously called "Theory X." Traditionally, it had been assumed people did not like work, needed to be coerced to produce, and responded to directive styles that included some threat of punitive options. He showcased the newer "Theory Y," a humanistic management approach in which people have potential to be committed to objectives without coercion but, rather, through a mix of rewards for achievement and the possibility of personal satisfaction. With the appearance of what McGregor termed as "Theory Y" in the 1960s, people became more fully enfranchised as participants in a company's success. They also started to be rewarded for that success as well.[11]

We see how a leader becomes a nexus for everybody's power in entrepreneurial business models that are highly regarded today. Take Dwight Carlson, CEO of Coherix. Carlson has been described as an "'entrepreneurial leader' who has learned how to create an environment that fosters innovation, hard work, a sense of fun, and 'team spirit,' one which results in a highly motivated and productive staff."[12]

Carlson said, "We are a group of professional entrepreneurs. This is our third industrial technology company. We are doing this because we love it; and you have to love it, or it will kill you. It's just brutal, but I love every minute of it. . . . It's fun, especially the third time, because you can anticipate what is going to happen."[13]

Carlson expresses an expectation for employees to display the same passion and dedication. "First of all, it's recruit the people. . . . Second, it's create, promote, develop, train the culture. . . . Can I force [team member A] to work very hard? No. I can create an environment where he knows he's being treated extremely well, highly respected. . . . I can't even stop him from working so hard. So, if you create the right environment, people motivate themselves. How long does it take to learn how to create that sort of environment? It took me thirteen very hard years to learn."[14]

Speaking of leadership vulnerability, take Tony Hsieh, the CEO of online shoe company Zappos. His bond with his employees played out over time, translating directly into memorable, unrivaled service and customer loyalty. His force as a leader made him an important nexus for his own staff and for all his stakeholders, from loyal customers to the very man who succeeded, despite Hsieh's resistance, in buying Zappos.

That leadership commitment has been a constant through challenges and rough waters. Through the ups and downs of leading Zappos, Hsieh remains committed to maintaining the culture that supports his people. With a plan to grow sales to $1 billion by 2010 and eventually go public, in August of 1999, Hsieh invested $500,000 in Zappos. The following year Zappos was out of money, but Hsieh decided to keep funding the company. Faced with the need to lay off half the staff, he reduced his salary to $24,000. His people, rather than being demotivated by the layoffs, produced an unwavering performance that is now the renowned Zappos quality brand. By 2005, gross merchandise sales were $370 million, and Zappos made the Inc. 500 list. In 2008, Zappos met the $1 billion goal.

The Zappos story doesn't end there. The company had relied on asset-backed credit to buy inventory, so when the recession and credit crash happened, its investors were hit hard, and Hsieh reluctantly sold Zappos to Amazon.com. Nonetheless, the bond between the leader and his people was not abandoned. Hsieh maintained his philosophy of investing in employees to foster better service, which created loyal customers who, in turn, drove long-term profit and fast growth. "We put our company culture above all else. We'd bet by being good to our employees—for instance, paying 100 percent health care premiums, spending on personal development, and giving customer service reps more freedom than a typical call center." In negotiating the acquisition, Hsieh conveyed his values and Zappos' vision to CEO of Amazon, Jeff Bezos, who permitted Zappos to continue operating independently. Hsieh stayed on as CEO at a salary of $36,000 per year. He remains dedicated to fostering a motivated workplace. Some practices include happy hours, tracking employee relationships, and offering $2,000 incentives for dissatisfied employees to quit. Hsieh commented on post-acquisition Zappos, "We have close to 1,800 employees now, and I think we're proof that a company doesn't have to lose itself as it grows bigger—or even after it gets acquired."[15]

Last year, LivingSocial CEO and cofounder Tim O'Shaughnessy[16] spoke to a large group of business leaders, including a large surge of young entrepreneurs seeking inspiration for their own aspirations of success. One of the region's fastest-growing companies, LivingSocial had already grown to more than 1,200 employees and 174 markets worldwide since launch a year earlier, and at the time was adding about six new employees a day. O'Shaughnessy, a young superstar, had already been named to the *Washington Business Journal's* "40 Under 40" and Inc.com's "30 Under 30" lists. LivingSocial had earned its kudos for the Hottest Venture Capital Deal award from the largest technology association in the country. He stood in front of the audience in the unassuming dress of a whole new era focused entirely on achievement without trappings. As we look into the future, that's worth remembering.

CHAT WITH AN EXPERT: DR. SHARON FLINDER

Sharon Flinder's work in advising clients is focused on leadership and organizational effectiveness through personnel retention, job satisfaction, performance measures, and strong communication. The wealth of wisdom she has to offer also draws on her own determination to be a lifelong learner.

"When we tell people it's everybody's business, we're not just telling them everyone is accountable for outputs and objectives. We're also implicitly insisting that everybody is responsible for how well internal communication and relationships function.

"What we find is that, despite a wealth of talent and knowledge in organizations, people hesitate to take advantage of what other people know. I can appreciate that some people feel it is safer not to. But they're missing out on important lessons someone else has paid to learn. They could be each other's best coaches. Sure, performance reviews may involve 360-degree feedback and training, but what about the informal way everyone has of reviewing each other's work? People usually don't want to have the kind of conversations that lead to real feedback. They don't ask each other the questions that could really help with their development.

> "Getting a lot of really smart, strong-minded people to collaborate can be difficult, but these are the best kinds of teams to drive a project forward—and they are the kinds of people who will set aside many of their own reservations if faced with a challenge whose solution advances the greater good. It's all about capturing mind and heart." —Sharon Flinder

"Not only to do people not ask for feedback, they don't want to give others feedback. Executives shy away from open conversations about strengths and weaknesses, performance, mitigators for weaknesses, goals, even a career path. Asking someone 'What do you want to do? What's next? How can we get you there?' can be a pretty intimate conversation. People are just not that readily disclosing. Then, everyone wonders why talent walks out the door. Well, nobody felt like they belonged—when they really did! And everyone regrets the cost of turnover, recruiting, and on-boarding.

"Any of us can be a leader in our own right, even though we're not nearly as perfect as we want to be. Of course, coaching is valuable, if only because, in a safe place, you get to admit you're not perfect. Also, it helps having someone to talk to in confidence. There's value from the conversation and from not having to hide or pretend. Sometimes you want to use an outside coach, but frequently colleagues make great coaches."

There it is, again: the dialogue among people. We've been considering the full creative dialogue needed for your organization to function smoothly. When I asked Sharon about the dynamic conversations she has seen at work, she answered, "Usually, there are pockets of culture where people are supportive, and this contributes to effectiveness; and then there are pockets of culture where people are not supportive, and all hell breaks loose. This is very much influenced by the leader. I've been at big meetings where people threw each other under the bus. Someone would publicly blame another person. When clients ask me why one problem or other persists with all its negative effects, I ask the hard questions about what the person did to model or enable the behavior involved.

"Having a 'burning platform' or sense of emergency can cover a lot of problems—for a short while. People unite under that urgency. At some point, however, the adrenaline runs out. That's when it's harder to unite people. But it's back to modeling. To foster a sense of purpose, the leader has to start by being inclusive. It's not about whether you like people more or less;

that is natural and it happens. What matters is that everyone is treated with equal respect and their potential for contributing is welcomed with equal regard. There's no real middle ground on whether a leader is magnanimous. She either is, or she isn't, and that affects how everyone approaches the dialogue with her, and within her purview."

So, what's the secret sauce, in Sharon's opinion? "It's a leader's basic job to keep people connected. He's not off the hook just because he may not see his team every day. If everyone were on the same hall, there's [Winston] Churchill's idea of walking around. The guy can just walk around and say 'good morning' to everyone. If the workforce is spread over different locations, he can find ways to make sure people feel remembered by him. From a phone call to an email to a Skype invitation, any leader can make any employee feel like she's on the radar. What is needed is a commitment to relationships and open communication."

Another way of looking at it: Sometimes, indeed often, you're the nexus. This is a good start on modeling the behavior for everyone around you.

ASK YOURSELF

Are you dubious about the time, energy, and money required to invest in workforce development? If so, here are some questions for serious consideration:

1. Does my organization have clear, communicated education, training, and development plans in place?

2. Are all individuals, including me, improving both professionally and personally?

3. Is our approach to workforce development driven by a customer focus?

4. What is the cost of one poor decision? One unresolved conflict? One weak work relationship? One disengaged leader?

5. What are my strengths and areas I can develop further? And can all employees answer this for themselves?

6. Do individuals know how to move forward to improve themselves and their situations?

7. What will I think, say, and do to make a difference? What are other individuals willing to think, say, and do?

6

PUZZLE: CREATING A SMART HUMAN CAPITAL STRATEGY

Smart businesses do not look at labor costs alone anymore. They do look at market access, transportation, telecommunications infrastructure and the education and skill level of the workforce, the development of capital and the regulatory market.
—*Janet Napolitano*

L et's telescope in from the full circle of your stakeholders to focus solely on the people you employ. Now that you have built bridges to connect with the real potential of individuals who participate in the creative dialogue, you can start to manage human capital as a resource. What this should mean is that you're assembling a kind of jigsaw puzzle using talent for pieces and a strategic plan for the box top. (This is definitely an exercise where you do not want to take on the vexing challenge of creating a puzzle without a box top illustrating the completed picture!)

Or you can think of the orchestra. Remember, there's a wide

range of instruments and musicians to piece into a whole according to a single score. You can't know what you need until you know what you have. Chances are that with a little extra tutoring or practice, many of the performers may be up for whatever challenge they face. In other words, you may have a lot more talent than you notice at the first rehearsal.

In human capital management, there are many tools at your disposal for assessing what you have. There are many methods for developing people to match the plan. There are, however, few strategic plans that align with the human capital issues you face.

Cost-effective human capital management makes sense as long as it happens within the context of a great plan and serves larger objectives. Good human capital strategies blend situation appraisal, background research, and needs analysis to assess your organization's current workforce circumstances. They produce solutions that focus on workforce alignment with short- and long-term strategies while implementing plans to support succession, on-boarding, and talent development. Some of the measurable effects of such strategies are staff satisfaction, engagement, and retention. The many approaches include one-on-one coaching, executive workshops, training seminars, advancement, and succession plans. Individuals and teams can enjoy and benefit from the focus of this kind of development. There are fundamentals at work in human capital strategies, and tried-and-true options exist.

What isn't optional in this idea-and-innovation economy is managing human capital as a top-line resource. If you want results, you need the best human capital management skills possible. You either have these skills or you hire expert skills. The experts either provide a short-term infusion or become imbedded in your organization to uphold the human capital endeavor. No matter how well you manage human capital or how you choose to incorporate the process into your business, human capital strategy is doomed to be just one more plan—indeed, just one more empty ritual—unless it plays out in a vibrant cultural dialogue that motivates, inspires, and magnifies greatness in all your people.

Remember 2+2=5? As you devise a human capital strategy, you are aiming for the multipliers. You want to plan for the ineffable quality that gets you to a sum of five when you start with two and two. What is that? The best human capital management professional may have theories, but ultimately no one individual can provide that surprise extra, the multiplier.

That's because people magnify each other. As the Hawthorne Studies found in the early twentieth century, bonding among people has a magnifying effect on productivity and even a quotient of happiness. These days, the team may entirely colocate in the same office or be connected across time zones and continents. It doesn't matter whether people share projects or knowledge. What matters is that they share the dialogue and exchange the ideas. They thrive in the dynamic. People in a successful dynamic do more in ways that are leaner, faster, better, and smarter. That's exactly what you need in today's economic climate.

We all see shifting environmental drivers, tumultuous

innovations, and advancing technologies that can undermine a stable and able workforce. The best and brightest talent is in high demand despite the weak job market. There's large-scale attrition from retiring baby boomers, and many new college graduates lack the skill sets needed for immediate employment. Human capital, that underpinning of all the production in an Ideas Economy, is itself churning and unpredictable.

Human capital risks can manifest themselves in different ways. One is the sheer lack of knowledge and leadership depth across the organization. Or there can be a protracted and unclear development path for entry- and journey-level staff. There can be poor alignment of talent to priorities and strategic objectives. One of the greatest risks is when nobody is talking to each other about possibility, knowing, and change.

The best-case scenario is that you find all the pieces to complete your puzzle. You have all the right instruments and musicians to execute your particular concert score impeccably. The worst-case scenario? Ultimately, your current talent mix proves unable to support the long-term objectives of your organization. So your first question when it comes to your talent mix must be, "Do I have enough of the right people in the right places performing the right work at the right time?" The immediate follow-up question must be, "Will I have that in five years?"

My answer to either question is another question. Who's talking about what? There's one proven way to make sure the dialogue in your business isn't idle chatter or bitter grievance motivated by boredom. What's that? It's collaboration. Of course, collaboration, while an art in itself, still relies on the baseline art of dialogue where business is concerned. In the end, whatever drives the conversations that magnify the potential greatness of your team is exactly what you want people to be discussing.

Organizations can achieve stability and minimize risk by creating a plan for developing current talent, for ensuring succession during attrition, and for retaining and attracting the best talent possible. This is true for periods of transition and growth. It is also true for periods of economic strain. A workforce prepared by development plans is the most cost-effective and impactful investment leaders can make in gaining competitive advantage.

And remember that great challenges provide great opportunities to keep a great exchange of smart ideas fueling the creative dialogue in your organization—every day.

DIALOGUE AND UNITY

Dialogue creates unity, and dialogue sparks disagreement as well. One of the things that a free exchange of ideas in any business will predictably spark is conflict. That's because smart people won't simply agree. Many think aloud and contradict themselves as they do. Others use debate to improve their own reasoning. Moreover, people with different work and life experiences process the same issue from different perspectives. Various professional disciplines approach the same point from distinct angles. So, sure, dialogue can divide, and it can also enrich. It all depends on the quality of the conversation.

This is the principle behind growing efforts to assemble truly diversified workforces. Different ethnicities, genders, orientations, and varying schooling, professional backgrounds, and styles spell diversity, and diversity is wealth when it's able to flourish. No matter how diverse a group or how much debate is going on, what ultimately makes things work is the unifying force of a shared ownership in outcomes. With that in place, conflict and differences can improve results.

Unity is forged in the same dialogue that expresses differences. This dialogue is not simply a corporate communication that is one-way. It can be a single idea, or it can be a common purpose. What matters is that in the end, everybody knows they own the outcome—good or bad—together. There have been many ways leaders have created unity in the exchange of ideas that also sparks discord and discomfort. The results have been remarkably similar. Here are a few examples.

Nothing unites people like ideas. Great ideas are the best connectors. A striking example of how the exchange of ideas can bond participants with enthusiasm and even debate is Wikipedia. Jimmy Wales, cofounder of Wikipedia, rallied thousands of people who are scattered around the world with a singularly appealing vision. He wanted an online, open encyclopedia. It would be everybody's encyclopedia, and the little non-profit start-up collected ideas and facilitated contribution and debate—all the way to billions of entries as of this writing. With his passion for sharing knowledge, Wales really knows what he's talking about when he speaks of what it was like "harnessing the power of lots of people who believe the same thing."[17]

Values unify, as long as people know them and incorporate them into the dialogue. Peter Brabeck-Letmathe, Nestlé's chairman and former CEO, was committed to aligning Nestlé's values with its culture. Describing Nestlé's culture as dynamic, open-minded, and multicultural because of its global reach, Brabeck-Letmathe said, "We do not have a Swiss culture or an American culture. We have a Nestlé culture, which is proprietary, and no one else has a similar culture. We have deep respect for the individual cultural background of all our employees, but we expect that they are willing to share our values." Brabeck-Letmathe even published the Basic Nestlé Management and Leadership Principles to create a solid starting point for hiring managers as well as organizational training. His belief was that, as long as the Nestlé values were clearly part of the dialogue, performance quality would remain constant across all cultures and nations where Nestlé did business.[18]

An employee-owned Canadian company, CGI is very clear about the power of its unifying principle—what CGI calls its "dream." The CGI dream is based on values to which the company is profoundly attached. CGI credits the unifying power of this dream for how its worldwide team of extraordinary and diversified talent has been able to build its own company. Rooted in the original and simple idea that first motivated CGI's founders when they created the company, the dream is simply articulated on the CGI website: "To create an environment in which we enjoy working together and, as owners, contribute to building a company we can be proud of." There is no doubt that CGI considers it to be everybody's business to know and grow the enterprise.

In his work *Jack: Straight from the Gut*, Jack Welch attributes his astounding success to being able to evaluate and develop talent. Welch claimed that, while GE was in many different businesses, he was in the "people business." He kept people focused on results and kept measurement criteria clear. His culture was based on accountability and teamwork. People were expected to participate in dynamic debate and to be able to make a strong case for their ideas. When asked about how he established such a rigorous meritocracy, Welch pointed to profit sharing as both a means of rewards linked to performance and a degree of ownership in the full business. Welch's performance rewards made GE everybody's business.[19]

In 1969, Dr. J. Robert Beyster, with a small group of scientists, founded Science Applications International Corporation (SAIC), which is now a FORTUNE 500® company with approximately 41,000 employees worldwide. SAIC rightly boasts of its employee-ownership philosophy that fuels an entrepreneurial spirit. Indeed, Dr. Beyster's commitment to the power of employee ownership in entrepreneurship led him to establish the Foundation for Enterprise Development (FED) in 1986. The foundation helps governments and private organizations use entrepreneurial employee ownership as an effective social and economic strategy. Later, in 2002, the nonprofit Beyster Institute for Entrepreneurial Employee Ownership was launched as part of the foundation. Now part of the University of California, San Diego, Rady School of Management, the institute promotes global entrepreneurship, employee ownership, and economic development through consulting, training, and international projects.

Forty years later, there's Steve Case. Case, most widely known as cofounder of America Online and retired chairman of AOL Time Warner, has spent recent years building a variety of new businesses through his investment company Revolution. Revolution is seeking to create "disruptive, innovative companies . . . that are attacking large, traditional industries with innovative new products and services."[20] Steve Case is actively seeking the disruptors, the discomfort makers, the change agents. He wants them as partners for the future. Case has boldly moved the discord in the industry dialogue front and center—as a source of hope.

When Case and Steve Gunderson addressed the Council on Foundations' Family Foundations Conference on January 30, 2006, in Honolulu, Hawaii,[21] Case took the idea of human capital management outside the walls of even the largest corporate setting. He explained to his audience, "We live in a world that is increasingly networked, interlinked, and interdependent, where old divides of boundary and belonging are getting blurred. We're seeing the way cooperation across barriers of distance and culture is bringing about advances inconceivable not long ago. Likewise, we need to expand perceptions of how to engage in philanthropy—to bring in new actors and forge new alliances that leverage our collective abilities."

In turn, Case said, the private sector will welcome this new collaboration. "There's no logical reason why the private sector and the social sector should operate on separate levels, where one is about making money and the other about serving society," he said. "Today's executives understand that in order for their enterprises to thrive and grow and attract the very best talent, they need to be able to draw on a healthy, well-educated workforce; offer safe, clean neighborhoods to prospective employees; sell to consumers with high enough levels of income to buy their products; and conduct themselves in a way that is attractive to shareholders' eyes. And that means, today, the business of business is social engagement as well."[22]

Steve Case sees community service as a human capital management strategy. He takes the sense of ownership and entrepreneurship to a broader dimension. While welcoming disruptive innovation, Case definitely falls into the corner of the power of partnerships, which is akin to appreciating the power of collaboration and dialogue. Recently, Case delivered a keynote address to an audience of powerful leaders and entrepreneurs in Northern Virginia at a sold-out event. That morning, I was inspired when I heard him say that his focus is to "invest in people and ideas that can change the world."

So the question for you remains: Are you prepared to be a dynamic partner? Are you ready to partner with your employees, your vendors, your investors, and your community? If so, that's excellent! You're setting yourself up to thrive in the future economic realities, which are upon us already.

CHAT WITH AN EXPERT: VAUGHAN LIMBRICK

Vaughan is one of the most creative group facilitators I have encountered. As a human capital strategist, she excels with the toughest audiences. Her decades of professional experience in the trenches of organizational transformation are colored by having run her own small and successful business.

"Think of it from the point of view of a person being managed," Vaughan replied when I asked her how she sees leaders maximize talent. "An effective leader makes you feel bigger than you were before your conversation with him or her. You might start the conversation seeing yourself in a 5x7 photo frame, but after talking with a masterful leader, you see yourself in an 8x10 frame—or larger.

"With a strong plan for managing human capital, we get groups functioning much better simply by adjusting the match. The people who come early, stay late, and won't complain about the money are the ones who find joy in the work. Some time ago the Center for Creative Leadership evaluated performance within job assignments and found that the person who does well is the person whose strengths match the job assignments. The person who doesn't do well is the one who doesn't have that match. It sounds obvious, but mapping out the talent to the work takes some smart strategic thinking. Many leaders have fallen prey to the crush of daily work and undermine the best way they have to improve performance—by working with the resources they already have!

> "I like to challenge groups to improve counterproductive habits groups often share by a collective contract that asserts: We can all share in the achievement if we are, from the start, willing to admit and voice the problem, be accountable for our role in creating the problem, expressing openly how we each need to change, agree to a course of action in which we are determined none of us will fail, and admit from the start the real consequence for failure. 'Are you determined enough to turn to our boss and say that, if you don't deliver on time and on budget, you'd fire yourself?'" —Vaughan Limbrick

"Implementing these strategies is another thing. There's the plan and there's the rollout; these happen in different ways. What is the same across the board and what determines the success or failure of the whole effort is the leader's willingness to communicate—not just the plan, but also at every step along the way. That's how an effective leader does exactly what he or she is supposed to do. The leader's role is to influence a diverse group of people to come together and execute a whole vision, one step at a time.

"I see the visionary leader thriving in this role. The styles range greatly. What they all do, in their own ways, is see possibility and broker hope. Even in leaders whose abilities are still diamonds in the rough, there is an innate sense of what makes the person in front of them tick, and how to work with that. This makes them possibility thinkers. They see each person as a possibility and go for that. I see that as an instinctive emotional intelligence, the kind of intelligence that uses dialogue to create a heart-to-heart bond.

"Management that works with the heart also learns with the heart," Vaughan continued. "This is a far cry from what I call 'management by lawyers.' What I mean is a view that a person gets a job description and works within the margins of that page; there is no expectation to see beyond that rectangle. A leader who offers this starting point in the creative dialogue you're talking about is just teaching people how to be disengaged from the greater whole. In fact, it's signaling each person to switch off curiosity and imaginative restlessness. In that kind of setting, I'd expect to see a lot of turnover in all the wrong people.

"The alternative to the boxed-in worker is someone thriving in a dynamic setting where leaders help their talented workers match strengths to challenge. Now, this kind of person needs to be comfortable feeling that they're in a constant learning mode. This setting naturally weeds out the few people who really are not motivated by the chance to be recognized for contributing smart ideas and great work.

"The impact of a great dynamic isn't limited to individuals, but rather the leader is adept in creating well-rounded work teams that collaborate for the best results. It looks a lot like TSI's interdisciplinary teams, actually, only the work assignments are more fluid. This kind of team grabs the vision and runs on the energy of possibility."

As we were talking, Vaughan commented how the best human capital management plans use real work projects and solutions to existing needs as the way to develop staff. "Savvy human capital management doesn't happen outside the work-flow. For example, I once convinced a client to tackle the adversarial culture she had inherited in a promotion by doing some leadership training as part of a larger annual gather-ing. What I did was devise a project in which small working groups each solved a problem facing their new boss, looking at it from her point of view. It was a real "eureka" moment for most of the people. They hadn't thought beyond their some-what insulated group in a long time. What really catalyzed lasting change was how colleagues, who were usually pitted against each other, actually were able to discuss calmly all the angles the leader should see. They ended up talking about the entire institution and found out they all shared similar values and longer-term goals.

"Before any of that new, positive capital could have a longer-term effect, though," Vaughan remarked, "it fell to the client to turn coach. She was either going to step up or miss the mark during those meetings. She really needed to use the opportunity to get to know each person enough to begin a dialogue that would last as long as she led that group. She did. Her success was fabulous."

ASK YOURSELF

Are you tentative about launching a human capital strategy initiative with so many priorities competing for your time and attention? If so, here are some questions for quiet contemplation:

1. Is an effective performance management system in place and understood by all employees?

2. Do employees have knowledge of the results their actions produce?

3. Do we have a full complement of strategies to initiate, direct, and sustain desired individual and team behavior?

4. Do we have enough of the right people in the right places performing the right work at the right time? Will we in five years?

5. How many key people are likely to retire or leave in the next five years?

6. What strategies will entice my best people to stay?

7. Are we motivating staff with career paths?

OPTIMUM: SUSTAINING PRODUCTIVITY WITH PASSION

Good enough never is. —Debbi Fields

A compelling issue for many of us is productivity. Organizational assessments look for it. Strategic planning targets it. An array of methods and tools improve and measure it. Talent and performance sustain it. When all is said and done, leaders seek to optimize productivity even when aiming to balance it with other factors such as quality, effectiveness, and innovation.

As a goal, optimizing productivity is as old as the first effort to produce some idea in multiples. Over the centuries the effort to optimize productivity evolved into a science and an art. There's no shortage of mechanisms and tools that claim to help.

Contrary to all the claims and promises by promoters that their mechanisms are the answer, what really counts in productivity is judgment. The mechanisms you choose depend on good judgment. The interpretations of results you obtain rely on your judgment. The optimum reflects not just the process of developing it; it also reflects the quality of your decisions while getting there.

The new realities in our economy demand that we do more with less. They push us to new levels of productivity. You can be sure they test just how effective a value stream map or a lean six-sigma scorecard really is. Indeed, today there's a cauldron where all the technical mechanisms for optimization are tested—by fire. This is true for the system and for each expert. There's zero tolerance for all-talk, underwhelming results. That's a good thing. Bring it on.

While mechanisms need to be chosen carefully, the real secret is you. To optimize productivity, you definitely need to know the tools at your disposal—as well as their shortcomings—in helping you achieve your goals. You may or may not engage experts to provide credentials and experience to tailor tools and methods to your circumstances. What you cannot afford to do is fall back on a formulaic, cookie-cutter approach. If you want a vibrant organization, make sure your process is vibrant, too.

The best mechanisms can enable good decisions. All the best decisions grapple with opportunity costs. In the best of circumstances, your decisions involve choosing from among several realistic options, almost all of which have some opportunity cost to pay. That's the point. Productivity is improved in one area often at the cost of resources to another. I'm talking about the strategic trade-off. Take a look at *Collins English Dictionary,*

Complete and Unabridged, tenth edition, which says that "optimum"[23] refers to a "condition, degree, amount, or compromise that produces the best possible result."

Resources are limited, so when you're ready for compromise, you're ready to optimize. You can create a production process where there was none and produce a design-to-delivery wonder like the Joint Mine Resistant Ambush Protected Vehicle Program, in which the US Marine Corps, working with the US Army, acquired armored vehicles in response to the deadly improvised explosive devices employed by the enemy in Afghanistan. They proceeded to deliver more hardware to theater faster than any previous effort, including World War II, which held the previous record.

Or you can step into an enterprise resource planning (ERP) rollout with over seven thousand users and retrofit a strategic training and support program requiring minimal additional investment and providing optimal utilization from launch onward.

In the first example, a strategic plan was formulated before the product was designed or the process was constructed, so opportunity costs involved investment in speed and quality to begin saving lives as soon as possible. In the second example, a strategic plan with a smaller scope was enhanced as the corrective action began, ensuring that the billions of dollars committed to technological upgrades don't get lost the moment staff is asked to begin using an unfamiliar system.

These two examples are among countless others available today. Launching new or upgraded product lines for tomorrow often generates chaos, resistance, or even stalemate in organizations. Meanwhile, new challenges occur rapid-fire, not waiting for groups to catch up. Operational environments change quickly and frequently, requiring constant adaptation for both your organization and your customers, who often need products with multiple configurations. Without a holistic process in overall alignment, individual acquisition components grow isolated and start to work more at cross-purposes, driving activity without achieving milestones. Are you certain you can provide new or upgraded product immediately at best value?

In its work with national defense programs, TSI has developed a process to create effective operational life cycles for new and upgraded products. With unique focus, we tap the talent and expertise of all stakeholders, forging from the start collaborative bonds among individuals and groups. Our work becomes a model for new product line management, integrating all aspects of a complex environment in what becomes a clearly mapped system of activity, role, and cost.

Yet our work in specialties like product line management, process improvement, and planning best-value products (among many others) have taught me an enduring lesson. Yes, our methods are tested and solid. Yes, our measurement tools are reliable. But direction will waver without a working plan. And decisions will flounder without good judgment.

Good decisions? They need reasoned trade-offs to keep productivity at its constant best.

Even optimal processes can begin to erode. Your functional teams, with their fast-paced workloads, tend to create processes in silos just to get the job done. The unintended effect of their dedication is that systems grow more complex. Activities start to become redundant. Waste emerges. Optimization is not just an initiative, it is also a way of being for any enterprise determined to succeed.

By looking at your organization as a total system, you can be sure to catch the redundancy, the complexity, the waste, and the development of silos before it's too late. You're best armed with a holistic approach that integrates processes across an organization, achieving substantial gains in efficiency and effectiveness—and staff morale. Does your organization have a routine discipline of continuous process improvement to maintain efficiencies? If not, do you really believe you can think yourself out of the box you thought yourself into?

Much is made of lean six-sigma and other methods for optimization. We have highly credentialed experts at our company who are specialists in lean six-sigma, but the first thing they will all tell you is that the downfall of lean six-sigma is, like most methods, when it becomes formulaic. At that point, the method leads while business realities are overshadowed. Even the methods for optimization used by mathematicians, scientists, economists, and engineers can be too mechanical to be optimal. To be optimally effective, they need to trade off some precision to factor in the power of human motivation and creativity.

That's why this book, which is all about encouraging you to recommit to process, product, and service excellence, talks mostly about things other than optimization. Those other things are real-time and continuous organizational assessment, big-picture thinking and strategic planning, and communication management at all levels. These are foundational elements that have a real and lasting effect on the productivity in all organizations—including yours.

As I've already asserted, agility is a requirement for today's realities. Structure and alignment define how agile your response to changing circumstances can be. When structure reflects the greater vision without contorting it, an organization is on its way to achievement. When roles, work, goals, and direction are aligned, an organization can face any challenge with lightning speed and unrivaled product design, quality, and delivery. Not only are organizations able to track accountability with accuracy, but employees are also better able to focus on priorities and key outcomes. Swapping complexity for simplicity leads to unconstrained productivity.

DIALOGUE AND INTEGRITY

When I see successful efforts to optimize production—or to regroup after failures to optimize—I notice a recurring theme. Sometimes it's front and center, sometimes it's a marginal note or implicit in the story, but what always happens is that dialogue is restored.

I'm in the business of optimizing productivity. Productivity relies on dialogue. Organizational assessments, strategic plans, implementation tools, and performance measures only do part of their job if they fail to take dialogue to the next level.

Another way to look at it is this: To be effectively used, strategies must be clear. That's true. Goals must be achievable. That's true, too. On top of that, any effort to drive productivity, including the profit or savings it creates, will fail in the long term unless there's dialogue to keep the business goals grounded in reality.

Consider the masters of production efficiency—Toyota. Akio Toyoda, president and CEO of Toyota, sat before Congress to speak about his company's failure to address design flaws in their production of many Toyota models. In prepared testimony before the US Congressional Committee on Oversight and Government Reform, Akio's regrets focused on how Toyota put business expansion goals over product quality. The customer, Akio acknowledged, had been placed second to expansion goals. Toyota had chosen the wrong trade-offs, with disastrous ends. Its business dialogue had turned inward, indeed, become insular.

Something Akio said remains with me as a note of hope. Akio spoke about how Toyota was beginning to grapple with their mistaken compromise of quality and brand in favor of growth. The company was admitting it put customers after leadership. I find in this cause to hope that Toyota can participate in the revitalization of Japan after the 2011 earthquake. Having a renewed focus realigned with the principles that led postwar manufacturing to greatness, Akio spoke of listening as part of the needed turnaround:

> Frankly, I fear the pace at which we have grown
> may have been too quick. I would like to point out

here that Toyota's priority has traditionally been the following: first, safety; second, quality; and third, volume. These priorities became confused, and we were not able to stop, think, and make improvements as much as we were able to before, and our basic stance to listen to customers' voices to make better products has weakened.[24]

The well-known story of IBM over the past three decades or so shows how process can undermine even market leaders. It also shows how a recommitment to dialogue can be the linchpin in any turnaround. In 1984, IBM was the number one supplier of microcomputers.[25] It owned 41 percent of the personal computer market. Within about a decade, its market share dropped below 7.3 percent.[26] In less time after that, IBM surged back to the forefront of the market again, and its share price increased seven times.

This astounding dip in IBM's market dominance can be seen as a failure in its product and distribution, which were both decentralized and hard to control. This low point provided, however, an opportunity for market leadership to be restored with dialogue as the driving force. According to Lou Gerstner, the CEO credited for reversing IBM's slide, "What IBM lacked was not the ability to foresee threats and opportunities but the . . . ability to integrate systems to solve customers' business problems."[27] Gerstner's strategy was to transition IBM from a traditional hardware provider into an impeccable service-focused company. The focus shifted from beating competition to serving clients' needs. IBM had moved into dialogue with its customers, and that became a brand identity. That return to the basics of customer satisfaction put Gerstner and IBM on the cusp of the wave that saw technology shift into service-based productivity, even where hardware is involved.

Customer dialogue faces additional challenges when it crosses national lines. No one knows how important cross-cultural dialogue is better than John Pepper, former CEO and current chairman of the board for Procter & Gamble. Pepper speaks about an effort to optimize P&G's profitability on an international scale that backfired for lack of dialogue. In the 1990s, P&G decided to standardize the Always brand by making packaging all one color. Immediately they lost significant business in China but had no idea why until they started to ask people. Consumers in China apparently base product recognition on color. So P&G adjusted their packaging to serve the consumer, not the bottom line, as the first priority.

Speaking of this eye-opening introduction to cultural sensitivities, Pepper says he now visits customers himself when possible. What he relates reveals how we who serve a market really can be motivated by serving our customer base. Pepper explained, "When P&G began in the nineteenth century, we were providing basic hygiene for people in a way that we in the United States can take for granted now. . . . You go into the homes in China or Russia and you see people using the first shampoo they've ever used . . . you come away feeling like you really need to deliver a good product."[28] He concludes that "the path to globalization is littered with the debris of companies that tried to treat all customers everywhere the same."

Choosing targeted actions for the biggest impact requires strategic insight and planning. Take David Haines, CEO of Grohe, a manufacturer of premium kitchen and bathroom fixtures. Haines knew sales were lackluster despite high-value products. His team took a careful and comprehensive inventory listening to their first-tier customers, that is, to distributors, such as retailers and wholesalers, that sold Grohe products along with competitors' products. Haines was looking not just for how to improve the chain of sale but also for what he could focus on for the most impact.

In response to distributors' ideas, Haines developed a marketing strategy to supercharge demand. He sent frontline sales reps into the field more often to promote continuous service dialogue, and he provided teams offering targeted marketing support to the distributors and even to the consumer base. Other initiatives included product installation workshops in distributor showrooms, new floor and window displays, and incentives to high-volume distributors. It was in this program that Grohe concentrated its resources. The trade-off decision had been made, the opportunity cost paid.

The Grohe program is a showcase for how financial objectives can be a beacon for bold business moves. Early in the program, analysts at Grohe could track a six- or even seven-point growth in revenue correlating to only a 10 percent improvement in NPS (net promoter score), a customer feedback metric.[29]

Innovation itself draws inspiration from keen awareness about what customers—or potential customers—have to say about any process. Take Bill Conner, cofounder of Alcon Laboratories. Alcon Laboratories became a 1960s success story when Conner exploited an incongruity in medical technology employed for cataract operations. As one of the world's most common procedures, the system had become routine and safer, except for one "old-fashioned" step of cutting a ligament. "Doctors had known for fifty years about an enzyme that could dissolve the ligament without cutting. All Conner did was to add a preservative to this enzyme that gave it a few months' shelf life. Eye surgeons immediately accepted the new compound, and Alcon found itself with a worldwide monopoly."[30]

Maybe the most enduring example of the power of dialogue with stakeholders at all levels is found in the iconic Nike crisis, when public outcry resulted after media profiles of the sweatshops in the company's supply chain. Dialogue was able to revive a brand to reach a whole new level of customer loyalty. At the outset, before the scandal broke, Nike outsourced production to independent suppliers, with the majority located in developing countries. It reportedly had little knowledge of poor working conditions, safety, or pay issues in supplier plants when public outcry erupted. At that point, Nike embarked on some corporate soul-searching, deciding to extend the scope of its responsibilities beyond its own employees to the system. Nike developed a strategic code of conduct that extends employee standards and monitoring systems to franchises and suppliers. Using its unrivaled buying power as leverage to improve working conditions in subcontractor and supplier organizations, Nike now has adopted ethical supplier conduct as a corporate obligation.[31]

Productivity relies on dialogue with stakeholders at all levels. That dialogue is about numbers and concrete goals. Open communications with all your stakeholders allows you to set ambitious targets to drive initiatives in your own enterprise to optimize productivity. Then again, my view of the best use for financial measures is reflected in how the chief financial officer at our company does his work. At a recent all-employee off-site retreat, business trends were presented by scholars, not the CFO. The business literature review was delivered by an intern, not the CFO. Then our resident "numbers expert," a.k.a. the CFO, closed this annual "strategic advance" with a motivational speech. At TSI, we not only believe numbers can motivate. We are motivated by numbers that focus on productivity. And we aren't the only ones.

CHAT WITH TWO EXPERTS: PAUL ODOMIROK AND DR. PATRICK HARTMAN

Paul Odomirok is a lean six-sigma master black belt who mentors green belts and black belts, and he specializes in tailoring lean six-sigma methodology to customer needs. Paul has played a key role in research into workplace productivity at Harvard, and he is a prolific writer.

I was discussing with Paul how important dialogue is for sustaining optimum productivity, and he offered many examples to prove the point. "I once worked with a leader who overtly violated numerous basic leadership principles. He primarily used fear to motivate people, and despite his rise as an emerging hero of the company, he destroyed the cultural fabric and framework of the organization. He excelled in delivering short-term results, but over the long term he could not maintain effectiveness due to the loss of commitment and support of the people. It was not only due to his leadership style, but because he drove the people to produce through fear, they closed down and became uncomfortable talking openly and frankly with him. Since he didn't provide a clear direction, consistent alignment of resources, and positive motivation, the people in the trenches were reluctant to provide feedback, ideas, and advice. There was no way that someone who pushed so hard in that manner for short-term results could understand and appreciate how the system operated, the true value of the people's input, and the real dynamics of his own segment of the value stream. He often duplicated efforts by placing several individuals on the same project in an attempt to create inner competition to create a superior solution. Resources were wasted, people became demoralized, and although short-term gains were realized, long-term success was negatively impacted. The workers burned out, shut down, drifted away, and left."

Based on the work of John Kotter, Jack Welch, Peter Drucker, James Kouzes, and Barry Pozner, I use ten primary points to evaluate leader effectiveness:

Five Actions:

(1) Setting direction

(2) Aligning resources

(3) Motivating people

(4) Communicating messages

(5) Executing the plan

Five Behaviors:

(1) Modeling the way

(2) Inspiring a shared vision

(3) Challenging the process

(4) Enabling others to act

(5) Encouraging the heart

—Paul Odomirok

"During times when there's a sense of urgency or a burning platform, leaders can leverage the emotional energy to move the organization forward by challenging and focusing that energy on the direction, purpose, and vision required. When an organization is in crisis, there is a propensity within any group to change. A perception of loss, or a fear of failure, is often present and mature leaders can leverage this condition to emotionally engage everyone and reconnect them with the collaborative sense of purpose and set them on the pathway toward success. But as the burning platform passes, you're often left with the questions of how to sustain change and how to continue to avoid oncoming wrong turns.

"I know it's often overused, but Toyota is a classic example of a success story that emerged from near dissolution in the late 1940s. Over the past seventy years, the company instituted fundamental change in the way it managed itself and produced its products. As a result, it emerged in the twenty-first century as a number one car maker. Some of its ultimate success became its problem, as it took its eye off the ball of its inherent strong sense of purpose and solid cultural foundation. Its recent crisis situation actually served to reconnect the culture with much of what it stood for, and assisted in revitalizing some of the long-time standing practices of listening to customers, suppliers, and every stakeholder of every type.

"You know, it can sometimes take a business at least ten years to recover once it stops adapting and evolving, and the best check-and-balance for avoiding extinction is to welcome feedback from all stakeholders. You must listen to customers, to suppliers, and to everyone, especially to each other. People don't think they have the time to listen carefully, but in actuality, they'll lose a lot more time in the long run when the business loses direction and has to spend a whole decade getting back on track."

When I asked Paul about the critical importance of listening, he explained that a great example of listening to the value stream occurred in the early 1990s when he was director of quality for NCR's retail systems division. Through the influence of Bell Labs, the company sought to incorporate every person into the design of its products, from customers to suppliers to investors to personnel. As a part of this initiative, division leaders spent two hours every Friday on what was called, 'Quality Tour.' Starting at the front end of the system with receiving, walking the process through production, and closing with the end of the system at shipping, the division's executive team visited with, and listened to, each process team's fifteen-minute status out brief on their performance.

"We paid attention to what they were saying, how they were doing, and what they needed to be successful. Afterward we met as a team to take that feedback and address what needed to be done to improve. In fact, the same tour was used to expose customers and suppliers to the system for the purpose of gathering additional feedback for improvement from upstream and downstream participants. We'd often have three to five customers come in each week to participate in our Quality Tour, expose them to how we built the products that we were shipping to them, and provide an opportunity for them to express any concerns or share any ideas that they had. We even communicated via satellite with shareholders in an all-hands meeting from the manufacturing floor. It was quite a bold partnership and everyone loved it."

Soon after speaking with Paul, I asked Pat Hartman about business leaders sustaining improvements to process, product, or service. Pat has a clear and enlightened perspective on any enterprise transformation challenge that he encounters. Pat had a few memorable comments from his own extensive experience with the US Navy.

"In government, the constant changes in the political environment make it seem like work must be tumultuous, but that's not the case. Looked at the right way, the underlying fabric of government is pretty constant. Operations continue, and they continue to need maintenance, upgrading, and improvement.

"There are similar changes in industry. Take technology. Personal computers, cell phones, GPS, apps, so many things have changed how people communicate. But the same principles underlie the communications. Business systems are taxed to keep up while they upgrade, but basically what makes it all work are the values in play as we communicate—however we do. It's up to leadership to live those, and the best way to model those values is by staying in a constant dialogue with people about what they are doing and what's the best way forward.

"It's not just about competence. That is very important. Competence depends on a leader's abilities in clear planning, understanding the environment, and coming up with inspiration on what to do about it. You've got to be able to benchmark similar businesses to see where they relate.

> "What you're looking for in leadership for today's innovative imperative is the person who can get teams motivated beyond what they could have done themselves. There's a special mix of high standards, humanity, and adaptability to that unique talent. The tools and the training can improve your people, but only a leader can unleash their best potential." —Pat Hartman

"Ultimately they communicate the values in their actions, too. Actions are part of the dialogue. Leaders motivate by being motivated. They energize others because they are energized themselves. What leaders can't do is make other people leaders. Leaders are self-developed. I think you can identify up-and-coming leaders and give them tools and training, but they're basically going to drive themselves to some high standard, or they won't. The really successful leader is able to get groups to new levels of success and then maintain that productivity, because they know how to communicate up and down the environment. There's always someone external to the group who's demanding that things be done. There are people who report to them who've got roles and functions to fulfill. Leaders need to be able to have meaningful dialogue with each level up and down this group—and sideways with vendors and other stakeholders—if they are going to be really informed with everything they need to know to sustain a long-term success. It's simple, but it isn't easy."

ASK YOURSELF

Are you wondering if committing to a standardized and continuous improvement process would be worth it? If so, here are some questions that provide food for thought:

1. Do we routinely integrate processes across the enterprise to maintain efficiencies?

2. How can we focus every resource and wellspring of talent on delivering customer value?

3. What value streams really drive my enterprise's success?

4. How do we know what outcomes our customers really value?

5. How do we inspire all staff to connect directly to creating customer value?

6. How do we monitor cross-organizational processes?

7. Do we have performance issues, process problems, or both?

8

ODDITY: FACILITATING TECHNOLOGY-DRIVEN TRANSFORMATION

Information technology and business are becoming inextricably interwoven. I don't think anybody can talk meaningfully about one without the talking about the other. —Bill Gates

Someone will, no doubt, justify a staggering investment in a new information technology initiative by promising upside for the bottom line at your organization. If you hesitate, you are in growing company. Customer dissatisfaction with enterprise resource planning (ERP) initiatives remains stubbornly consistent year to year. Indeed, the sad discovery in the current state of things is an embarrassing downside to enterprise technology improvements. They can undermine productivity and profit.

A quick take of some basic statistics reveals that the business trend is to pause before investing further in enterprise technologies. The Forrester Group, a reliable market analyst, predicts that 2011 expenditures for ERP solutions will be flat or will slightly decline. Of the 900 ERP users surveyed, few have plans to upgrade or invest in the current ERP system. They are simply completing their existing initiatives. Over half the companies have admitted that planned releases lag sorely behind schedule.[32] Why spend more with implementation stalled?

In another survey, from 2008 to 2010, dissatisfaction with the pace of ERP rollout rose from 35.5 to 61.1 percent of all executives and staff surveyed. Over half of all end users, who worked at all levels in businesses surveyed, complained that the current ERP solution was underutilized. The consensus was that the technology was operating at 50 percent or less of its promised capability. Each year of the survey, 40 percent or more of the respondents complained about work being disrupted. As if that's not troubling enough, the same number criticized the process for not having provided a way to cope with the backlash impact that new technology had on the organization and its human capital, following rollout.

What these individual customers say reflects a troubling conundrum for our nation. On the one hand, new technologies can supercharge innovation and really sharpen a competitive edge in organizations. This holds true for your business and mine as well. Moreover, organizations have evolved into networks of stakeholders. Most vendors, many employees, and countless others who are involved in productivity work outside the traditional bricks-and-mortar setting. Our enterprises can no longer function without new technologies that make us unified. Truly, he who hesitates to use technology is lost in a networked, global world.

On the other hand, new technologies disrupt productivity (for longer periods than expected). That promised upside seldom materializes. So, in a world where hesitation is very risky, what's funny—in the sense of being very odd, but far from amusing—is that hesitation has become a smart technology strategy for many organizations. These statistics voice a troubling conventional wisdom. It can be smarter to fall behind than to disrupt business by implementing the latest technological innovation.

Let's face facts. While organizations sit on the sidelines, hesitant to employ bold IT solutions, the global economy surges forward. New national economies shift into leading roles. New threats are emerging as adversaries devise ingenious new tactics. Our competitors are riding the wave of technology, often with more aplomb than we.

Don't worry. A moment of discovery in this story is upon us. It's finally dawning on people that a great enterprise technology upgrade requires a plan.

What really happens is that some customer somewhere realizes it's time to seek a strategy outside the scope of the technology launch. For us at TSI, that appears as a call from a customer who is disgruntled with how her enterprise technology initiative is going and is asking us if we can get an effective plan together like the last one we facilitated.

When that call comes our way, we swiftly help build or enhance a strategic plan, jumpstart implementation management, and drive the initiative toward the goal, with everyone trained and motivated to achieve performance benchmarks plus receiving ongoing support. What we do for our customers, you can ask your management consultants to do for you— or you can explore strategic solutions on your own initiative. Alternatively, some organizations provide situational enterprise transformation solutions by tapping internal leadership for temporary projects.

With all due respect to the technology leaders, great and small, who drive our economy, they are sometimes the least able to provide the business overhaul required for their own technology overhauls to flourish. So, when customers turn to their technology partner for a fix or for guidance, they may be talking about problems encountered in the enterprise technology discussion when business process issues are really what's at stake. That's why an objective third party, with total systems improvement acumen, can help everyone by adding assurance that the technology specialist relies on an enterprise transformation strategist to keep expertise at its highest value for the dollar.

No matter the source, however, a strategic transformation plan is needed. The goal is clear: to deliver on the promise of payback on investment, the new technology must be fully utilized. How does this happen? Productivity changes one person at a time. Full technology utilization happens one person, one user at a time.

This is why enterprise technology initiatives such as enterprise resource planning are not simply technology projects. They are change management on a personal level. They rely as much on creative performance benchmarks and measurements as on sound programming logic. Think of it as making your human capital and business processes as bug-free for implementation as you expect your technology expert to make the software.

This idea flips typical enterprise technology launches upside down. That's because you typically see large enterprise IT systems launched top-down. The change that ensues from the rollout quickly can outpace the organization's capacity. Work is disrupted across the enterprise. The implementation process comes to be about survival, not learning or growing.

By engaging all stakeholders—from the bottom up, from idea through launch—your IT solution will be as useful as you hope from the start. Better, the technology gets more useful with each new day and each new challenge. Buy-in and usefulness are only two reasons stakeholders must be involved in this kind of enterprise-wide initiative. You also protect yourself from simply codifying outdated or flawed core business processes in your future!

Don't be one of the many, many leaders who discover late in the game that your IT enterprise solution is, de facto, an overhaul of your business. Decisions with lasting impact will be made on the fly. The statistics bear me out. Inadequate delivery on utility includes not just poor training; it suggests systems that constrain the organization from adapting to a changing environment and programs that are more suited to the technologically savvy than to those who are savvy in delivering your products or services.

There's a way to confront these challenges head-on. We have found success using an outcomes-driven approach to launching technology transitions. We mix elements of organizational assessment and strategic planning with developmental training to ensure all features of the new technology have meaning in daily work life. It's the best way to protect your enterprise from costly, demoralizing disruption.

This approach can flourish in a balanced partnership between a minimalist, performance-focused strategy and a technology-focused design. Here's the key to customer satisfaction in IT programs: All stakeholders must be included. Performance measures must be established. Every single person must know what is expected of him in using the new software, what it can provide, and how it links to his functional responsibilities. Your people know the strategic thrust of the investment and the financial goals. Each person becomes, to recall the opening of this book, Eva, a person able to protect the organization from disruption thanks to a keen understanding of the greater picture and of how all the systems can work for individuals and those around them.

DIALOGUE AND TECHNOLOGY

Technology is central to innovation. It relies on innovation, and innovation relies on technology. The two are inextricably inter-woven in the process of discovery, whether that's discovering the makings for early computers or discovering the new orga-nizational designs possible only with advanced, high-powered enterprise technologies.

What most engineers consider the very first computer is

now on the famed IEEE Milestones list. The Atanasoff-Berry Computer, or ABC, existed in prototype as early as 1939 and included stunning functions like electronic computation, binary arithmetic, parallel processing, and a separation of memory and computing functions. For years, the inventor had puzzled over vexing issues until, inventor John Vincent Atanasoff recounted, key principles dawned on him in a sudden flash after a long wintry drive one night. It took until 1942 for Atanasoff to build the functioning ABC with the help of a graduate student, Clifford Berry, in the basement of the physics building at Iowa State University. Challenging thinking proceeded the "eureka" moment, and hard work followed.

That moment of discovery, however, is sometimes overshadowed by all the hard work of thousands of people who participate in creating strategy and implementing designs, like the one spearheaded by a young company, NCR, where another precursor of the modern computer was inadvertently being developed.

During World War II, the US Navy set a goal to design a processor that could decrypt German U-boat messages faster than the human mind. The discovery process that followed was less straightforward than a drive on a cold Iowa winter night. The navy ran teams in three shifts per day, staffed by some six hundred WAVES (Women Accepted for Volunteer Emergency Service), one hundred officers and enlisted men, and a large civilian workforce. A very young company called NCR[33] took the lead in the technological innovations. The first high-speed processing decrypting machine, known as a "bombe," was tested in May 1943. A month later, two fully functioning bombes were able to crack a particularly impenetrable German code.[34] The goal had been attained.

People celebrated the watershed, but more work had to be done. In short order, they produced another 119 bombes. Approximately 3,000 people set to work decrypting German U-boat messages day and night. The US Army, too, had followed a parallel path, relying on Bell Labs for prototypical telephony, and one result was the faster push buttons that we associate with telephones.

Whether between two partners or within a large team with many moving parts, technology and innovation must continue to fuel a creative exchange in all our organizations. That dialogue is part happenstance, with the discovery as an outcome. It also requires strategic guidance. Without that, technology, like all large-scale business process overhauls, might improve productivity, but no one will know. And, when no one knows, most people default to assuming technology is the enemy.

Consider how the dialogue worked against the army, even as it was launching a hugely successful IT initiative. Since first deploying to 4,000 users in July 2003, the logistics modernization program (LMP) delivered impressive results. It now manages $4.5 billion in inventory. It processes transactions with 50,000 vendors and integrates data with more than eighty Department of Defense systems. Meanwhile, the LMP has continued to sustain large legacy systems. With this unusual success, the LMP faced a serious challenge. Most users considered it a failure at delivering on its promises.

On review, the people running the rollout of the LMP realized they had failed to establish a strong dialogue with all stakeholders. They had not clearly described the phases of implementation, and they had not returned routinely to give progress reports and listen to peoples' problems. As a result, support fell off among all management levels soon after first launch. Even though the system consistently exhibited superior performance according to metrics for the technology itself, people believed it was failing expectations. The metrics had failed to wed personal performance to performance on the new technology.

Today, Army G4, Army Materiel Command, and Program Executive Office Enterprise Information Systems (PEO EIS) are in regular dialogue with internal customers as well as other stakeholders in the army and defense communities. Progress reports are measured against planned expectations. The sense of customer satisfaction has been on the upswing.

Speaking of the experience, Col. David W. Coker wrote, "Communications in such circumstances are crucial when you take into account the natural resistance users feel on being asked to give up a homegrown system to learn new processes required by an ERP. . . . They thoroughly understand the old systems, and even as they curse the old system's shortcomings, many users have come to judge themselves as experts in its use. And there is a certain level of comfort, confidence, and pride inherent in that attained expertise. The implementation of an ERP solution will upset this apple cart. This is where an active change management, communications, and outreach program becomes necessary."

The centrality of linking technology to human performance metrics has reached critical mass in new business organizations that bear the mark of high-tech enterprise systems. Jeremy Seligman, who is now the director of information technology strategy and organizational development at Ford Motor Company, described his work on the Edison Project when he began as a consultant at the company. The Edison Project aimed to reform the IT infrastructure of the entire company. Where the IT group had mostly operated in a fragmented structure, serving distinct groups that were having more and more trouble exchanging ideas and integrating work across divisions, the Edison Project developed a total systems approach. They started by bringing key stakeholders together to diagram Ford's infrastructure using causal loop diagrams and stock-and-flow computer models to help better understand interrelations. "Once the team understood what the costs and benefits would be to the entire system," Seligman said, "it was easier to make the case for change to everyone who would be affected."[35]

Seligman credits the success of the Edison Project at integrating groups to the fundamental exercise of increasing members' appreciation of the larger picture. With that perspective, all stakeholders were more open to making changes for the benefit of the greater whole. What happened was that individuals and groups found it much easier to exchange creative ideas and participate in dialogue at many levels. Technology had been successfully tapped for greater enterprise integrity—through dialogue.

No business model better reflects the exciting potential

impact of technology on the other side of a successful IT enterprise program than AT&T, which emerged from its turnaround with a whole new organizational identity.

"Net-Centricity" is the term coined to describe the implementation of a new concept of business continuity across AT&T's global structure. Pointing to its long history with telework and new technology rollouts, John Kern, director of disaster recovery at AT&T, explained that AT&T has long been "a company organized around networks rather than buildings . . . with business continuity and telework part of the natural blend."[36]

Net-Centricity works for AT&T because it has a solid intranet in place, a web-based process for home office provisioning, and the expectation that all AT&T managers are proficient remote managers. With fluency in this model of work, AT&T has positioned itself to offer organizational preparedness initiatives—business continuity planning (BCP)—as the scalable process for advance development of arrangements and procedures that allow organizations to respond to emergency events so that critical business functions continue with minimum interruptions in the event of a crisis. Telework is the cornerstone of AT&T's business continuity strategy and of its BCP for other organizations. It's also how many people work for many businesses today. Nothing underscores the need for excellent strategic planning for IT programs that make or break productivity like all those that support the increasing number of teleworkers in the United States. For example, at the time AT&T was rolling out Net-Centricity, it reported employing 22,500 teleworkers, with 17 percent of staff being virtual office workers and 40 percent being part-time teleworkers. It could also boast significantly reduced absenteeism and $180 million saved per year resulting from increased productivity and reduced real estate costs.[37]

The dialogue in other industries runs along similar lines. It's hard to talk about the impact of technology on our business innovations without mentioning its undisputed role in the future of our economy and nation. A few industry leaders have been raising similar issues that are worth sharing here.

In his recent speech to business leaders in the northern Virginia area, Northrop Grumman chairman, CEO, and president Wes Bush explained that the defense industry will be faced with a loss of innovation and increased competition without an aggressive push to strategically manage the defense industrial base. At the helm of one of the great forces in the region's economy, Bush expressed a very real concern that "the dynamic range of threats facing our nation and its interests is unparalleled in our history." He also expressed his belief that the lack of new-start programs will have negative consequences on the ability of the defense industrial base to build and maintain critical skills in the future. To address these threats and challenges, Bush advocated for what I assert on a day-to-day basis: Investment and all other decisions need to be benchmarked against the clearly prioritized defense industrial capabilities that are most critical to the long-term security of the nation.[38]

Before a similarly large group of the same leaders, White House cybersecurity coordinator Howard Schmidt was invited to discuss current cybersecurity initiatives and the future of the government's cybersecurity strategy. What most struck me was how yet another national leader was advancing the idea that innovation and technology happen together. For Schmidt, that means more partnership with more dialogue and a greater exchange of ideas. Pointing to how cybersecurity is both a national security priority and an economic opportunity, Schmidt explained that government-industry partnerships are crucial because the vast majority of the nation's critical infra-structure is in the hands of the private sector. That makes cyber-security a shared responsibility across sectors and a driver behind dynamic partnerships in the near future. What stuck with me was the echo of my own reflections: The dialogue between tech-nology and innovation is what will keep the nation safe and drive its economy as well. At the heart of the matter? Dialogue.

Beyond the impact of technological innovation on the very structure of our organizations, and beyond its role in our nation's security, there is the future to consider. Speaking to an overflow crowd of business leaders in northern Virginia, Walt Haven-stein, CEO of Science Applications International Corporation (SAIC), shared his reflections about his own passion—inspiring the next-generation technology workforce.

SAIC, one of the fully employee-owned companies in the region, commits time and treasure to supporting science, technology, engineering, and math (STEM) education under Havenstein's leadership. Discussing STEM programs such as FIRST, for which he serves as chair, Havenstein explained that students in high school STEM competitions and activi-ties, as opposed to those in high school sports, are much more likely to "go pro" in their field. Concluding his remarks, he highlighted the Northern Virginia Technology Council's Equal Footing Foundation, which supports computer clubhouses for underserved youth, and encouraged all companies to engage in STEM initiatives such as those at the Equal Footing Foundation and FIRST.

As he spoke, Havenstein placed the onus on the leaders sitting in the ballroom listening that morning. "There aren't enough of us to sustain the growth our industry needs," he said, and the technology industry has a critical role to play in helping to inspire the next generation of innovators and inventors. Our economy and our nation depend on our stepping up and taking the lead in fostering talent for the future.[39]

CHAT WITH AN EXPERT: BRIAN SKIMMONS

Once a US Navy cryptographer with extensive experience in new technologies, Brian Skimmons also leads many collaborations with enterprise technology launches, so I wanted to be sure to talk to him about my reflections on the partnership between IT initiatives and strategic business planning.

"People have to understand the value of technology—not all technology, but this one particular mix of software and hardware that they will be responsible for. A lot of people think this involves pain, but not if you handle it from the right perspective. I look to get people jazzed about how software functionality actually links to tasks in their daily job. The harder the task, the more likely I can get them jazzed about how technology can make it a lot easier to do.

"Let's say you have an ERP underway. My goal is to get people aligned with how that software is supposed to move the organization. Training needs to start before rollout. You know, I'd rather start with some performance work before we train on the software. Some people resist the software because it really forces them to take stock of their own business habits and make changes. That's for the good, but it's not easy.

"Once you get intelligent people to where they have a good idea about the big picture, almost everyone is more motivated to participate in any change, including technology changes. You throw a few clear-cut objectives and performance measures into the mix, and you can really empower the professional and the supervisor to start a dialogue about how well the software is or is not working—and what ways the people involved can grow and improve, too.

> "I coach a youth baseball team. Now there's a group that's really interested in metrics. What they want to do is win, and that's what the numbers mean to them at the outset. But as they develop their sportsmanship, they start to see that the metrics of the game are a way to challenge themselves as individuals and as a team. Winning is a thrill, but the real results are revealed in the metrics." —Brian Skimmons

"The same goes for the business processes. You are going to find that the logic behind software design will be a great challenge for process improvements. It's a whole new use for lean six-sigma and some of the strategic value stream work we do. You end up with a picture. The picture is easy to understand. The brilliant techies and the focused business groups can all understand the picture. They stop talking different languages at each other. It's great."

Brian and I ended up talking about the impact of technology on organizations. Thinking of our business, we could easily talk about networked organizations, which have colleagues on teams that are sometimes far-flung, reaching internationally and around the country. "Or," as Brian noted, "you have the guy three offices down the hall who now prefers to fire off an email instead of picking up the phone or doing something really radical, like walking down the hall to ask you in person.

"That flattens out the organizational chart," he said later. "Technology has changed the nature of business from two decades ago, when there was a more established chain of command. Then, you didn't go talk to a boss's boss. Now you can email anybody; anybody can influence anybody else with a single email. That's a lot of activity either moving everyone forward—or distracting everyone from a baseline of productivity.

"It works for ERP planning, and it works for all our other customers. Outcomes come back to meeting goals and objectives successfully. There's no start and end; it's continuous. Leaders should be able to articulate and bring the organization together on agreed-upon objectives, and then you have to trust the people to meet the objectives, or you need to support people growing into those autonomous roles. It's not like we all work side by side anymore. The only way to track productivity uniformly is watching the outcomes, the results. That changes how people look at their own work, just as they have had to learn new ways to communicate beyond bricks-and-mortar offices.

"What's the first, best way I check whether people are going to be productive in this new setting? I just ask them to articulate their boss's objectives and challenges. If they can do that as well as they can describe their own, I know they understand the bigger environment. They're ready for great decisions. We can start at a whole new level when they can operate as productive individuals with a clear idea of where they fit into the system."

In other words, Brian checks to see if the people he helps move forward in enterprise technology initiatives arrive at the starting line with the expertise of Eva, our superstar server.

ASK YOURSELF

Are you lost in mystery about how to implement and leverage the best information technology solutions within your enterprise? If so, here are some questions for you to ponder:

1. Are my enterprise technology initiatives achieving full financial, operational, customer, and stakeholder outcomes?

2. How can we minimize work disruption at launch?

3. Will output improvements return our full investment?

4. How do we best align business processes and IT requirements?

5. Is there a clearly defined and communicated need to change to better IT solutions?

6. Do employees understand the importance of any technology transitions that we have planned?

7. Do we have a clear understanding of what the "best in class" are doing with respect to leveraging technology?

9

ENERGY: MEASURING AND MOTIVATING PERFORMANCE

One accurate measurement is worth a thousand expert opinions. —Rear Admiral Grace Hopper

My team excels in performance measurement. In fact, they're fanatics. At TSI, we don't want a plan to exist without tools for evaluating outcomes. We believe people have no business leading unless they are prepared to inspect what's expected of their people, of their product or service, and of their business processes.

You'd be in good company if you feel data-rich and information-poor. It's far too common for people to spend an inordinate amount of time collecting and reporting lots of meaningless data yet end up lacking what they need to make key decisions.

It's simple. The metrics you use to inspect what's expected must create the high-res info feed I mentioned at the opening of this book. There's your real-time, meaningful information.

That's what you need to align your decisions with the overall strategic direction of the business.

That's the same high-res info feed you can share with your stakeholders. That information can help make it everybody's business to know and to grow the enterprise. Everyone is given enough real information to align their decisions and work progress with the strategic direction made clear and simple in a living, inspiring, and bold strategic plan. Do you want to motivate your best people? Give them a clear plan, and make sure they know how to measure results. As George S. Patton said, "If you tell people where to go, but not how to get there, you'll be amazed at the results."

In our organizational assessments, we find ourselves taking the inventory of workplaces where the culture is deflated, defeated, or just plain nasty. What we hear are people complaining about not knowing what's important. Many don't even know if their performance is acceptable; they are working blind, in a way. When information is provided to them, it isn't relevant. Or it's too little, too late. Or it leads to decisions that inspire no confidence, because people don't have confidence in the data. This dilemma is common and crippling, because it tolerates a blind spot in everyone's activity. It drains the energy from each person's forward motion, because they grow wary and overly cautious. What they need to know are the results you expect and how everyone will know when people achieve them.

By contrast, the right performance measurement tools energize people. It helps them make decisions for success, and most people want to succeed. Metrics can drive innovation, sometimes in places where we doubt it's possible. Think about former mayor Martin O'Malley's initiative to push the city of Baltimore, Maryland, to use CitiStat, a performance-measurement data and management system. CitiStat permitted city officials to maintain statistics on everything from crime trends to the condition of potholes. It created a holistic picture of how policies and procedures were being implemented throughout a complex governmental system. That gave the city leaders clear data to evaluate and to use when prioritizing change efforts. It was, pure and simple, a performance measurement tool.

In its first year, CitiStat saved Baltimore $13.2 million.[40] Great ideas started to percolate among city staff, and innovations started to roll out in affordable, trackable phases. For example, mass transit innovated with hybrid fleets and real-time tracking at bus stands. Mobile data terminals in city vehicles now serve as communication hubs between vehicles and control centers, automatically sending data on location, passenger counts, engine performance, mileage, and other information.

This kind of holistic tool can manage shrinking budgets and distribute limited resources in a decision process that assures the greatest bang for the buck. It can get you to the point where the smallest step with the biggest impact is obvious. It's not just the data that makes that magic. It's the strategic clarity of a plan and the ensuing dialogue that foster the respectful exchange of ideas and creative possibility thinking.

In the savviest of companies, performance metrics for people and processes inspire dialogue about adjustments and adaptation. The performance review is more like a tune-up than a dress-down. It is regular, even daily sometimes, because leadership is a dialogue, not a meeting.

Evaluation proves promises are kept. It empowers talented people to set and achieve bold goals. Measurement tools are crucial to impeccable leadership, because they are reliable decision-making aids that showcase results and drive an adaptive culture. Evaluation measures provide evidence that resources are being used efficiently. They keep an organization honest through role clarity and inspire as well as reward great talent.

Funding depends on proving worth. That's as it should be. Investment seeks a measurable return. That's reasonable. When the process of measurement creates confusion, fear, or resistance, it undermines effectiveness. Complicated tools create data that is not broadly useful. Punitive dialogue over moving targets in performance expectations must be a thing of the past. Our organizations are too networked, and our external challenges are too daunting. We all need a steady stream of meaningful data and a clear bar to raise or change as we adapt.

Many tools and processes exist for measuring performance, and some are very good. Tailoring combinations that work for you can make or break your corporate culture—and your fiscal success. The details of your measuring practices aside, what I'll remind you to do is gauge the effectiveness of your performance measurement process and tools. Ask yourself this question: Do your employees leave the dialogue about inspecting what's expected of them energized and motivated? If not, you need a performance metrics overhaul, fast.

The best measurement is individual knowledge. The metrics are tailored to create a vital decision-making experience. When the question "What's important to us and how are we doing?" is asked, the answer is visible to everyone. People generally share the same conclusions, because they have the same information and the same goal.

When everybody understands how they fit into the big picture, amazing things happen. Timely, accurate, trustworthy, and complete information is available to help people answer the questions that keep them up at night. Members of the organization have an ongoing source of performance data, allowing quick responses to "unexpected" questions with little additional effort. People self-manage, and they experience this autonomy as the kind of freedom that inventors, innovators, visionaries, and forward-chargers need to be their best, to do great things, and to have meaningful success.

It really pays to approach measurement holistically. With a total systems view, even the most networked business, with teams whose members are not colocated at all, can thrive in the clarity. Multiple disciplines can be integrated into a rich force for change and productivity, much like the multidisciplinary teams that work at TSI.

There's one way to find that next best small step with the greatest impact for the smallest resource cost. That's to craft a clear strategy and plan, foster a bold dialogue among all stakeholders, and imbed smart metrics into your workplace so that, every day, it is everybody's business to know and grow your enterprise.

DIALOGUE AND TRUTH

Andy Taylor, the CEO at Enterprise Rent-A-Car, and his senior team decided to adapt the measurement criteria at Enterprise Rent-A-Car to assess customer loyalty every month, with a customer poll consisting of only two simple questions. One question asked about the quality of the rental experience. The other asked about the likelihood the customer would rent from the company again. Based on these questions, customers are categorized as "promoters," "passively satisfied," or "detractors." The clear categories were defined to help communicate results to front-line managers. With this simple, fast process, the leadership figured it could provide fast, real-time feedback to its 5,000 US branches. And it did.

Enterprise Rent-A-Car also used the data to study how customer responses related to actual purchases and referrals in the long term. It was discovered that customers who gave the highest rating to their rental experience were three times more likely to rent again than those who gave Enterprise the second-highest grade. The company used neutral and negative experiences for training and problem identification.

Managers were ineligible for promotion unless their group scores matched or exceeded the company's average.

Not too surprisingly, scores rose across the company. As scores rose, so did Enterprise's growth relative to its competition. The company considers the $4 million per year cost for the measurement system cost one of its best investments.[41]

Sabre, Inc., is the inventor of electronic commerce for the travel industry. At the forefront of its industry, Sabre restructured functional teams into virtual, cross-functional teams in 1999 in order to better serve their customers. Based on interviews with seventy-five executives, leaders, and virtual team members, the company identified performance measurement as the greatest challenge for the developing virtual company. Managers wanted to know how they could manage people they could not even see.

From this internal dialogue, Sabre developed a comprehensive performance metric that included team-level scorecards to assess quantitative data consisting of growth, profitability for each travel booking, time required to order and install customer hardware, and customer satisfaction. The metric built strong teams who were given the data so they could assess their own performance. Managers could monitor group communication archives to assess subjective factors such as idea generation, leadership, and problem-solving skills. Team members were even empowered to embark on structured peer review. Once this performance measurement system was put in place, even though team members hardly saw each other, Sabre's customer satisfaction ratings improved, its market share increased, and the number of travel bookings increased significantly each year.[42]

More locally, in northern Virginia, one of the firms designated among the hottest emerging companies is Smarthinking, Inc., which is committed to developing and delivering high-quality academic support programs with state-of-the-art technology. Smarthinking's education team members are seasoned educators with years of experience in online education. The team is dedicated to student success by hiring, training, and managing the best tutors available. Many education team members are also authors. With Smarthinking, students experience online tutoring that is simple, fast, and always available. Students connect to live educators from any computer that has Internet access, with no special software installation or equipment required. Smarthinking provides online tutoring twenty-four hours a day, seven days a week, enabling students to get the help they need when they need it.

Using an advanced queuing system requiring little or no wait time, students are connected on demand with an expert educator. Students work one-on-one in real time with a tutor, communicating via a virtual whiteboard technology. Scientific and mathematical notation, symbols, geometric figures, graphing, and freehand drawing can be rendered quickly and easily. Smarthinking even has an online writing lab, where staff help students at their point of need. So, how would you try to inspect those expectations after setting them so high?

Smarthinking, Inc., thought big, and that was smart. In 2011 it announced the completion of a study commissioned by the evaluation unit of the Division of Florida Colleges that examined the impact of Smarthinking tutoring services throughout the Florida State college system. The study's results confirmed the effectiveness of academic support from Smarthinking and of continued investment of federal College Access Grant funds for a third consecutive year to help subsidize college purchases of Smarthinking. Twenty-seven of the twenty-eight Florida State colleges currently use Smarthinking's services.

The study shows that among students who are taking either developmental education courses or first-level college courses in mathematics or English, those using Smarthinking's services received higher grades. College Preparatory Test (CPT) scores of study participants and nonparticipants were very similar, showing that the resulting higher grades do not appear to be a result of self-selection of only stronger students using Smarthinking's services.

"We are very pleased that Smarthinking has partnered with Florida's state colleges to make their services more readily available to our students," said J. David Armstrong Jr., president of Broward College. "We have found that our 'on-the-ground' and online students appreciate having quality tutoring available during the times when they need assistance, all with the convenience afforded by online access."

CHAT WITH AN EXPERT: DR. GARRY COLEMAN

Garry Coleman is a leader in the field of strategic performance measurement. Indeed, he was invited as one of the industry's bright stars to write the chapter on this specialty for the *Handbook of Industrial and Systems Engineering*.[43]

Garry, a dedicated volunteer in his home community, also spearheads work with the Marine Toys for Tots literacy program and TSI's STEM-friendly support of the Society for Engineering and Management Systems' best student paper competition for graduate-level scholars. Garry's cutting-edge work on the national defense community's counter-IED effort is most impressive, but what strikes me most when I have the opportunity to speak with him at length is how down-to-earth he is, and how much empathy he brings to his defense clients. His grounded common sense and colorful stories from his early years working as an engineer in coal mines contribute to a delightful aura of humility and wisdom.

"Effective leaders are servant leaders," Garry said. "They set direction and serve the people who work in order to get the business where it's supposed to go. Once they set direction, it's not their job to micromanage. It's their job to support and enable everybody else to achieve goals. Leaders make everybody else shine.

"A leader must be able to provide clear methods along with clear goals. If goals are arbitrary, people lose faith in the goal and in the leader who set them. Sure, I can tell you to aim for a 50 percent improvement, but is that even possible? The goal has to be credible to start and achievable at the end.

"It's the same thing with methods to get where you're going. Goals without methods lead to a lot of exertion and busywork, and rarely get the desired results. They do little but cause frustration and destroy morale.

"In the mining industry circa 1985, safety inspectors were required to inspect the underground work sites every eight hours, within a three-hour period prior to each shift. If they don't, the site has to shut down. At one site, the inspector could barely complete the inspection on time. Sometimes he was late. He was exasperated and claimed he was doing the inspections as quickly as he could. So we sent a young engineer to join him and evaluate the feasibility of our expectations for this inspection. It turned out that the foreman's goal, which originally had been reasonable, was no longer possible. That's because the site had grown a lot bigger. Of course it took the inspector longer to walk through the site. Not until we took a look into the performance shortfall did we see what was really in play. The foreman hadn't considered the impact of growth on this one man's job.

"Some goals just aren't possible without changing the methods or the expectations, so the metrics can't be one-dimensional. You can hold a gun to someone's head and get them to do what you want, maybe, for a brief high-adrenaline spurt. Does that make you a good leader? How many times can you get away with that? Strategy and metrics have to work together to sustain great performance for the long term.

"Employee success is an outcome. If you develop employees that people want to hire away from you, that's a good sign. Leaders should have goals aligned so employee success contributes to the organization's success. You can't have too much of one without the other. Employees have to grow and learn. Let them work with someone or do something they haven't before. Rewards should reinforce your values."

Listening to Garry, I had to chuckle, because he was talking about performance metrics, but he hadn't even mentioned scorecards, reviews, probationary periods, or hiring or firing. He kept talking about clear expectations and rigorous inspections of what is expected.

"Let me give you a last example. It's in the mining industry, again. A company I worked for would let us leave work early on Fridays if the week's quota was met. If you stayed after the quota was met, you got paid time and a half. Our management had aligned our goals—an early weekend—with their goal of a reliable outcome every week. Every choice we made was related to meeting the quota. We all wanted out early on Friday.

"Aligning goals among stakeholders is one purpose of good metrics. It's a great way to reward relationship-driven work. It encourages people to slow down enough to talk and listen and participate in impromptu negotiations to create solutions right away. Problems don't fester, because people don't procrastinate. Goals make time valuable and relationships even more valuable. There's a lot of good conversation going on in a business that relies on a solid measurement program for tracking performance. Even the most bureaucratic organization can take on a whole new vigor when a strategy is clear, goals are aligned, and people have the metrics to evaluate their own performance."

So, what does Garry think divides the leaders who can produce sustainable results from those who cannot? "I tell people to ask themselves this question: Do you have a farmer's mentality or short-term investor's mentality? Short-term investors typically want to maximize their money as soon as possible, sell promptly, and get out. Farmers are focused on the long term—this year and next year's crop and they want to pass a healthy productive farm on to the next generation."

ASK YOURSELF

Are you dreading the idea of gathering data, converting it into information, and portraying it to the right audiences? If so, here are some questions to help you move forward:

1. What categories of results best define our successful performance? Is this a balanced set of categories?

2. What indicators best reveal what is needed for consistent, top performance?

3. Would an independent third party commend our performance?

4. Do we have clear, line-of-sight measures that help individuals understand the connection of their results to organizational performance?

5. How do we justify requests for budget increases?

6. Do we have full support from our funding sponsors? If not, what additional information could be provided to engage them to be 100 percent supportive?

7. What are the right criteria for choosing sound action?

CLOSING REFLECTIONS

People usually get stuck dreaming about changing the world. What's really required is to believe you can change the future by taking the time to have personal impact on one life for a lifetime. —*Colleen Hahn*

Talk about everybody's business! My company retooled a few years ago to focus on one industry, defense, as a way to serve our military, whose leadership we hold in high regard. It also means we serve the country. We serve everybody. And we're proud to be part of the solution, making tax dollars work better, smarter, leaner, and faster.

I'm also proud to serve with a brilliant group of creative professionals for whom impeccable style and relentless discipline go hand in hand. With their remarkable talent and energy, they come to serve our customers every day with something indescribable—the strength of character and wisdom that come only from having met and prevailed over significant challenges in their own lives. As they bring the principles in this book to work for our customers and our community-service partners as a powerful working team, their personal integrity and professional humility comprise the foundation underlying the workplace transformation for which they are so often credited.

This epilogue can afford to be as compact as the book it closes. Most epilogues must sum everything up in order to deliver an uplifting, memorable idea the reader can take away. I don't need to. Your next best steps *are* the uplifting end of this book. You have every reason to expect to make giant strides toward the boldest goals you can imagine and to make it everybody's business to know and grow your enterprise!

ENDNOTES

1. http://www.hiltonworldwide.com/aboutus/commitmentaction. htm [accessed March 16, 2012].

2. M. C. Wilson, *Leaders in Motion: Winning the Race for Organizational Health, Wealth and Creative Power* (Arlington, VA: Transformation Systems, Inc., 2009).

3. http://www.businessinsider.com/ten-inventions-you-never-knew-had-inventors-2011-3#1959-a-picnic-lunch-inspired-ernie-fraze-to-invent-the-pop-top-found-on-soda-cans-1#ixzz1VxfXvxcx [accessed March 16, 2012].

4. http://www.businessinsider.com/ten-inventions-you-never-knew-had-inventors-2011-3#1986-twenty-somethings-scott-jones-and-greg-carr-bring-voicemail-to-people-everywhere-8#ixzz1Vxg4l5mE [accessed March 16, 2012].

5. Ikujiro Nonaka, "The Knowledge-Creating Company," *Harvard Business Review* (July 1, 2007); reprint # R0707N-pdf-eng [available at www.hbrreprints.org].

6. Henry Mintzberg, *The Rise and Fall of Strategic Planning: Reconceiving Roles for Planning, Plans, Planners* (New York: Free Press, 1994).

7. F. Stone, "Molson Coors 'Our Brew,'" *MWorld* (9): 17

8. Ibid.

9. Ibid., 19.

10. CNNLiving.com, April 9, 2011: http://articles.cnn.com/2009-04-02/living/cnnheroes.suezette.steinhardt_1_affordable-housing-family-preservation-permanent-housing/2?_s=PM:LIVING [accessed March 20, 2012].

11. Douglas McGregor, *The Human Side of Enterprise* (New York: McGraw-Hill, 1960).

12. D. Strubler and B. Redekop, "Entrepreneurial Human Resource Leadership: A Conversation with Dwight Carlson," *Human Resource Management* 49 (2010): 793.

13. Ibid., 799

14. Ibid., 796.

15. Tony Hsieh and M. Chafkin, "Why I Sold Zappos." *Inc.* 32 (2010): 100–104.

16. Keynote speech at NVTC Titans breakfast, April 6, 2011.

17. E. Corcoran, "The Answer Man," *Forbes.com*, Retrieved from http://www.forbes.com/forbes/2005/0905/122.html [accessed September 5, 2005].

18. K. Burrus-Barbey, "Leadership, Global Management, and Future Challenges: An Interview with Peter Brabeck-Letmathe, Chief Executive Officer of Nestle SA," *Thunderbird International Business Review* 42 (2000): 495–506.

19. Jack Welch and John A. Byrne, Jack: Straight from the Gut, revised edition (New York: Headline, 2003).

20. http://www.revolution.com/our-story/about-revolution [accessed March 21, 2012].

21. Ibid.

22. http://www.casefoundation.org/spotlight/business/webcast [accessed March 21, 2012].

23. Dictionary.com, "optimum," in *Collins English Dictionary, Complete & Unabridged*, 10th Edition. Source location: HarperCollins Publishers. http://dictionary.reference.com/browse/optimum [accessed: September 7, 2011]

24. "Toyota Swings to Profit Despite Recall Woes," CnnMoney.com, retrieved from http://money.cnn.com/2010/05/11/news/companies/toyota_earnings.cnnw/index.htm [accessed March 23, 2012].

25. P. Werhane, "Mental Models, Moral Imagination, and System Thinking in the Age of Globalization," *Journal of Business Ethics* 78 (2008): 463–74.

26. H. Chesbrough and D. Teece, "Organizing for Innovation: When Is Virtual Virtuous?" *Harvard Business Review* 80 (2002): 127–35.

27. Bruce Harreld, Charles O'Reilly, and Michael Tushman, "Dynamic Capabilites at IBM: Driving Strategy into Action," *California Management Review* 49, no. 4 (2007): 26.

28. C. Bingham, T. Felin, and J. Black, "An Interview with John Pepper: What It Takes to Be a Global Leader," *Human Resource Management* 39 (2/3, 2000): 289.

29. R. Markey, F. Reichheld, and A. Dullweber, "Closing the Customer Feedback Loop," *Harvard Business Review* 87, Dec 2009, 43–47.

30. Peter Drucker, "The Discipline of Innovation," *Harvard Business Review* 76, Aug 2009, 149–57.

31. P. Werhane, "Mental Models, Moral Imagination and System Thinking in the Age of Globalization," *Journal of Business Ethics* 78 (2008): 463–74.

32. http://candeos.com/erp-spending-in-2011-who-is-right/ [accessed March 26, 2012].

33. A. P. Mahon, *The History of Hut Eight,* 1939–1945 (1945), U.K. National Archives Reference HW 25/2.

34. Ibid.

35. J. Seligman, "Building a Systems Thinking Culture at Ford Motor Company," Reflections (2005): 6, 1–9.

36. www.workingfromanywhere.org/news/ITAC_Explore_
Telework.pdf [accessed April 23, 2012].

37. The Telework Advisory Group of WorldatWork, "Exploring
Telework as a Business Continuity Strategy: A Guide to
Getting Started," *WorldatWork* (2005), retrieved from http://
www.workingfromanywhere.org/news/ITAC_Explore_
Telework.pdf [accessed March 26, 2012].

38. http://www.northropgrumman.com/
presentations/2011/021111-wes-bush-securing-the-nation-an-
industry-perspective.html [accessed April 23, 2012].

39. http://www.nvtc.org/events/geteventinfo.
php?event=TITANS-32 [accessed April 23, 2012].

40. T. Perez and R. Rushing. "The CitiStat Model: How
Data-Driven Government Can Increase Efficiency and
Effectiveness," Center for American Progress Report (2007):
1–18.

41. N. Morgan and L. Rego, "The Captain Must Know the Ship's
Parts: The One Number You Need to Grow," *Harvard Business
Review* 82 (2003): 134–36.

42. B. Kirkman, B. Rosen, C. Gibson, P. Tesluk, and S.
McPherson, "Five Challenges to Virtual Team Success: Lessons
from Sabre, Inc.," *Academy of Management Executives* (2002),
16, no. 3: 67–79.

43. New York: CRC Press, 2005.

BIBLIOGRAPHY

N. Anand and Richard L. Daft, "What Is the Right Organization Design?" *Organizational Dynamics* 36 (2007): 329-44.

Virginia Anderson and Lauren Johnson, *Systems Thinking Basics: From Concepts to Causal Loops* (Massachusetts: Pegasus Communications, 1997).

Martha C. Andrews, K. Michele Kacmar, Gerald L. Blakely, and Neil S. Bucklew, "Group Cohesion as an Enhancement to the Justice-Affective Commitment Relationship," *Group and Organization Management* 33 (2008): 736-55.

H. Igor Ashoff, *Corporate Strategy: An Analytical Approach to Business Policy for Growth and Expansion* (1965).

AT&T Knowledge Ventures, "Making the Case for Enterprise Mobility: Remote Access Solutions," 2006, AT&T,

http://www.business.att.com/enterprise/exchange_
resource/Topic/networking-applications/Whitepaper/
making_the_case_for_enterprise_mobility_solutions/.

Larry Barrett, "Roadblock: Regional Managers," *Baseline* 54 (2006): 50.

Murray R. Barrick, Bret H. Bradley, Amy L. Kristof-Brown, and
Amy E. Colbert, "The Moderating Role of Top Management
Team Interdependence: Implications for Real Teams and Working
Groups," *Academy of Management Journal* 50 (2007): 544-57.

Brooke Bates, "Single File," *Smart Business Los Angeles* 5 (2010):
12-16.

Josh Bernoff and Ted Schadler, "Empowered," *Harvard Business
Review* 88 (2010): 94-101.

Chris Bingham, J. Stewart Black, and Tepo Felin, "An Interview
with John Pepper: What It Takes to Be a Global Leader," *Human
Resource Management* 39 (2000): 287-92.

"Biography," last modified March 30, 2005, http://www.sramanami-
tra.com/bio/.

Stephanie M. Bryant, Susan M. Albring, and Uday Murthy, "The
Effects of Reward Structure, Media Richness and Gender on
Virtual Teams," *International Journal of Accounting Information
Systems* 10 (2009): 190-213.

Katrina Burrus-Barbey, "Interview: Leadership, Global Management,
and Future Challenges: An Interview with Peter Brabeck-
Letmathe, Chief Executive Officer of Nestle SA," *Thunderbird
International Business Review* 42 (2000): 495-506.

Milly Casey-Campbell and Martin L. Martens, "Sticking It All
Together: A Critical Assessment of the Group Cohesion–
Performance Literature," *International Journal of Management
Reviews* 11 (2009): 223-46.

Luc Cassivi, Pierre Hadaya, Elisabeth Lefebvre, and Louis A.
Lefebvre, "The Role of Collaboration on Process, Relational, and

Product Innovations in a Supply Chain," *International Journal of e-Collaboration* 4 (2008): 11-32.

Phillip A. Chansler, Paul M. Swamidass, and Cortlandt Cammann, "Self-Managing Work Teams: An Empirical Study of Group Cohesiveness in 'Natural Work Groups' at a Harley-Davidson Motor Company Plant," *Small Group Research* 34 (2003): 101-20.

Henry W. Chesbrough and David J. Teece, "Organizing for Innovation: When Is Virtual Virtuous?" *Harvard Business Review* 80 (2002): 127-35.

Chun-Hsi Vivian Chen, Ya-Yun Tang, and Shih-Jon Wang, "Interdependence and Organizational Citizenship Behavior: Exploring the Mediating Effect of Group Cohesion in Multilevel Analysis," *Journal of Psychology* 143 (2009): 625-40.

CNN Wire Staff, "Toyota Swings to Profit Despite Recall Woes," CnnMoney.com, May 11, 2010, http://money.cnn. com/2010/05/11/news/companies/toyota_earnings.cnnw/index. htm.

"Coherix Wins $2.5 Million in Automaker Business," *Quality* 47 (2008): 11.

Amy E. Colbert, Amy L. Kristof-Brown, Bret H. Bradley, and Murray R. Barrick, "CEO Transformational Leadership: The Role of Goal Congruence in Top Management Teams," *Academy of Management Journal* 51 (2008): 81-96.

Elizabeth Corcoran, "The Answer Man," *Forbes*, September 5, 2005, http://www.forbes.com/forbes/2005/0905/122.html.

John L. Cordery and Christine Soo, "Overcoming Impediments to Virtual Team Effectiveness," *Human Factors and Ergonomics in Manufacturing* 18 (2008): 487-500.

Simona Covel, "Making a Virtual Company a Reality," *Wall Street Journal—Eastern Edition*, January 10, 2008, http://online.wsj. com/article/SB119991779050478949.html.

Wanda Curlee, "Modern Virtual Project Management: The Effects of a Centralized and Decentralized Project Management Office," *Project Management Journal* 39 (2008): S83-S96.

Christian Czipura and Dominique R. Jolly, "Global Airline Alliances: Sparking Profitability for a Troubled Industry," *Journal of Business Strategy* 28 (2007): 57-64.

The Datamonitor Group, "Allianz AG: Company Profile," Datamonitor, 2010, 1-10.

The Datamonitor Group, "American Express Company: American Express Company SWOT Analysis," *Datamonitor* (2010): 1-9.

The Datamonitor Group, "Charles Schwab Corporation: The Charles Schwab Corporation SWOT Analysis," *Datamonitor* (2010): 1-8.

The Datamonitor Group, "Molson Coors Brewing Company: Adolph Coors Company SWOT Analysis," *Datamonitor* (2010): 1-9.

Deanne N. Den Hartog, Annebel H. B. De Hoogh, and Anne E. Keegan, "The Interactive Effects of Belongingness and Charisma on Helping and Compliance," *Journal of Applied Psychology* 92 (2007) 1131-39.

Anthony DiPrimio, "The Managerial Mistakes that a CEO Must Avoid," *Journal of Case Research in Business and Economics* (2009): 21-18.

Matthew Dixon, Karen Freeman, and Nicholas Toman, "Stop Trying to Delight Your Customers," *Harvard Business Review* 88 (2010): 116-22.

Peter F. Drucker, "The Discipline of Innovation," *Harvard Business Review* 76 (1998): 149-57.

"Edward E. Whitacre Jr.," *New York Times*, June 9, 2009, http://topics.nytimes.com/topics/reference/timestopics/people/w/edward_e_whitacre_jr/index.html.

"Executive Profile: Edward E. Whitacre Jr.," *BusinessWeek*, last modified August 12, 2010, http://investing.business-week.com/businessweek/research/stocks/people/person.asp?personId=187888&ric=T.

Jane Fedorowicz, Isidro Laso-Ballesteros, and Antonio Padilla-Melendez, "Creativity, Innovation, and E-Collaboration," *International Journal of E-Collaboration* 4 (2008): 1-9.

Peter Fischer, Tobias Greitemeyer, Suat Ilkay Omay, and Dieter Frey, "Mergers and Group Status: The Impact of High, Low and Equal Group Status on Identification and Satisfaction with a Company Merger, Experienced Controllability, Group Identity and Group Cohesion," *Journal of Community and Applied Social Psychology* 17 (2007): 203-17.

Kimberly Furumo, "The Impact of Conflict and Conflict Management Style on Deadbeats and Deserters in Virtual Teams," *Journal of Computer Information Systems* 49 (2009): 66-73.

David Goldman, "How AT&T Gets Stimulus Funds: The Nation's Biggest Telecom Company Is Well Positioned to Get Stimulus-Related Projects Because of Its Reach with Government Agencies," *CNNMoney*, July 14, 2009, http://money.cnn.com/2009/07/14/news/companies/att_stimulus/index.htm.

Charles E. Grantham, James P. Ware, and Cory Williamson, "Chapter 6: The Virtual Workforce," in *Corporate Agility* (New York: AMACOM, 2007), 129-59.

Samuel Greengard, "Keeping the Customer Satisfied," *CIO Insight* 109 (2009): 32-35.

Wieslaw M. Grudzewski, Anna Sankowska, Monika Wantuchowicz, and Lukasz Babuska, "Process-Based Performance Measurement in a Virtual Organisation," *International Journal of Networking and Virtual Organizations* 4 (2007): 217-28.

Anthony W. Haddad, "The Vision and Confidence of Charles Schwab," *Equities* 57 (2008): 40-44.

Shakir Hafeez and SAF Hasnu, "Customer Satisfaction for Cellular Phones in Pakistan: A Case Study of Mobilink," *Business and Economics Research Journal* 1 (2010): 35-44.

John Hagel and John Seely Brown, "Today You Can Only Be a Leader by Creating Leaders," *Forbes*, September 22, 2010, http://www.forbes.com/2010/09/22/leadership-development-pull-leadership-managing-future.html.

Laura A. Hambley, Thomas O'Neill, and Theresa J. B. Kline, "Virtual Team Leadership: The Effects of Leadership Style and Communication Medium on Team Interaction Styles and Outcomes," *Organizational Behavior and Human Decision Processes* 103 (2007): 1-20.

Voss Hanswerner, "Virtual Organizations: The Future Is Now," *Strategy and Leadership* 24 (July/August 1996): 12.

J. Bruce Harreld, Charles A. O'Reilly III, and Michael L. Tushman, "Dynamic Capabilities at IBM: Driving Strategy into Action," *California Management Review* 49 (2007): 21-43.

Rick Holden and John Hamblett, "The Transition from Higher Education into Work: Tales of Cohesion and Fragmentation," *Education & Training* 49 (2007): 516-85.

Frank M. Horwitz, Desmond Bravington, and Ulrik Silvis, "The Promise of Virtual Teams: Identifying Key Factors in Effectiveness and Failure," *Journal of European Industrial Training* 30 (2006): 472-94.

Tony Hsieh, "Zappos's CEO on Going to Extremes for Customers," *Harvard Business Review* 88 (2010): 41-45.

Tony Hsieh and M. Chafkin, "Why I Sold Zappos, Inc.," *Harvard Business Review* 32 (2010): 100-104.

"Inspiring Innovation," *Harvard Business Review* 80 (2002): 39-49.

Michael C. Jackson, *Systems Thinking: Creative Holism for Managers*, (Chichester: Wiley, 2003).

Neera Jain, Anjanee Sethi, and Shoma Mukherji, "Impact of

Communication during Service Encounters on Customer's Perception of Organization Image," Paradigm 13 (2009): 56-65.

Lauren Keller Johnson, "Debriefing Barbara Kellerman: How Bad a Leader Are You?" review of *Bad Leadership: What It Is, How It Happens, Why It Matters*, by Barbara Kellerman, *Harvard Management Update* 10 (2005): 3-4.

Peter J. Jordan, Sandra A. Lawrence, and Ashlea C. Troth, "The Impact of Negative Mood on Team Performance," *Journal of Management and Organization* 12 (2006): 131-45.

Ron Kaufman, "In Challenging Times, Service Matters the Most," *Supervision* 3 (2009): 14-15.

Barbara Kellerman, "Leadership Warts and All," *Harvard Business Review* 82 (2004): 40-45.

Bradley L. Kirkman, Benson Rosen, Cristina B. Gibson, Paul E. Tesluk, and Simon O. McPherson, "Five Challenges to Virtual Team Success: Lessons from Sabre, Inc.," *Academy of Management Executive* 16 (2002): 67-79.

Stephen B. Knouse, "Building Task Cohesion to Bring Teams Together," *Quality Progress* 40 (2007): 49-53.

Stephen B. Knouse, "Task Cohesion: A Mechanism for Bringing Together Diverse Teams," *International Journal of Management* 23 (2006): 588-96.

John Kotter, *What Lenders Really Do* (1999).

James M. Kouzes and Barry Pozner, *The Leadership Challenge* (2008).

Michelle LaBrosse, "Working Successfully in a Virtual World," *Employment Relations Today* 34 (2007): 85-90.

Yi Lai and Brendan Burchell, "Distributed Work: Communication in an 'Officeless Firm,'" *New Technology, Work, and Employment* 23 (2008): 61-76.

"Leadership Team: Chistopher Rice," last modified 2011, http://blessingwhite.com/leadershipTeam.asp.

Robert C. Liden, Sandy J. Wayne, Renata A. Jaworski, and Nathan

Bennett, "Social Loafing: A Field Investigation," *Journal of Management* 30 (2004): 285-304.

Tom Lowry, "Can Tim Armstrong Save AOL?", Bloomsberg Businessweek, December 3, 2009, http://www.businessweek.com/magazine/content/09_50/b4159042686122.htm.

C. Lynch, "5 Things I've Learned," *CIO Insight* 20 (2007): 72.

Kenneth D. Mackenzie, "Process Skeletons and Functions," *Human Systems Management* 28 (2009): 201-12.

Joan Magretta, "The Power of Virtual Integration: An Interview with Dell Computer's Michael Dell," *Harvard Business Review* 76 (1998): 72-84.

Arvind Malhotra, Ann Majchrzak, and Benson Rosen, "Leading Virtual Teams," *Academy of Management Perspectives* 21 (2007): 60-70.

Maneesh Mehta, "Future Signals: How Successful Growing Companies Stay on Course," *Ivey Business Journal* 70 (2005): 1-7.

Manpower Group, "The World of Virtual Work Facts and Statistics," (n.d.), http://www.manpowergroup.com/press.

David Mantey. "I Drive a Toyota Yaris," *Product Design and Development* 65 (2010): 8.

Massimo Manzin and Borut Kodric, "The Influence of Outsourcing and Information and Communication Technology on Virtualization of the Company," *Managing Global Transitions* 7 (2009): 45-60.

MarketWatch, "Company Spotlight: Ford Motor Company," *MarketWatch: Automotive* 9 (2010): 15-21.

MarketWatch, "Company Spotlight: Harley-Davidson Inc.," *MarketWatch: Automotive* 9 (2010): 18-25.

MarketWatch, "Company Spotlight: IBM Global Services," *MarketWatch: Global Round-Up* 7 (2008): 326-31.

MarketWatch, "Company Spotlight: Nestlé," *MarketWatch: Drinks* 9 (2010): 31-39.

MarketWatch, "Company Spotlight: Procter & Gamble," *MarketWatch: Personal Care* 9 (2010): 21-27.

MarketWatch, "Company Spotlight: Toyota Motor Corporation," *MarketWatch: Automotive* 9 (2010): 29-38.

Rob Markey, Fred Reichheld, and Andreas Dullweber, "Closing the Customer Feedback Loop," *Harvard Business Review* 87 (2009): 43-47.

Elton Mayo, *The Human Problems of an Industrial Civilization* (1933).

Keith McFarland, "Improving Your Team's Learning Curve: Frequent Meetings that Focus on Successful Strategy Help Team Members Learn What Works," *Bloomsberg BusinessWeek*, http://www.businessweek.com/smallbiz/content/jul2007/sb20070717_389668.htm.

M. Mehta, "Future Signals: How Successful Growing Companies Stay on Course," *Ivey Business Journal* 70 (2005): 1-7.

Michael D. Michalisin, Steven J. Karau, and Charnchai Tangpong, "Leadership's Activation of Team Cohesion as a Strategic Asset: An Empirical Simulation," *Journal of Business Strategies* 24 (2007): 1-26.

Sramana Mitra, "New Ways to Mentor Entrepreneurs: Using Telepresence and Web Conferencing to Reach and Teach Entrepreneurs All Over the World," *Forbes*, November 11, 2009, http://www.forbes.com/2009/09/10/mentor-entrepreneur-cisco-intelligent-technology-telepresence.html.

Mitali Monalisa, Tugrul Daim, Fahim Mirani, Pranabesh Dash, Rabah Khamis, and Vijay Bhusari, "Managing Global Design Teams," *Research Technology Management* 51 (2005): 48-59.

Fiona Moore and Chris Rees, "Culture Against Cohesion: Global

Corporate Strategy and Employee Diversity in the UK Plant of a German MNC," *Employee Relations* 30 (2008): 176-89.

Neil A. Morgan and Lopo L. Rego. "The One Number You Need to Grow," *Harvard Business Review* 82 (2007): 134-36.

Nick Oliver, Matthias Holweg, and Mike Carver, "A Systems Perspective on the Death of a Car Company," *International Journal of Operations and Production Management* 28 (2008): 562-83.

Cecily Raiborn and Janet B. Butler. "A New Look at Telecommuting and Teleworking," *Journal of Corporate Accounting and Finance* 20 (2009): 31-39.

George E. Reed, "Leadership and Systems Thinking," *Defense AT&L* 35 (2006): 10-13.

Sarah Reynolds, "The Importance of Customer Service in Today's Economy," *Managing Imports and Exports* 2009 (2009): 14.

Christopher Rice, "Low Engagement? Invest More in Your People," *Leadership Excellence,* November 2008, http://www.eep.com/merchant/newsite/excellence100.htm.

Julia Richardson, "Managing Flex-Workers: Holding On and Letting Go," *Journal of Management Development* 29 (2010): 137-47.

Benson Rosen, Stacie Furst, and Richard Blackburn, "Overcoming Barriers to Knowledge Sharing in Virtual Teams," *Organizational Dynamics* 36 (2007): 259-73.

Benson Rosen, Stacie Furst, and Richard Blackburn, "Training for Virtual Teams: An Investigation of Current Practices and Future Needs," *Human Resource Management* 45 (2006): 229-47.

Lara Schlenkrich and Christopher Upfold, "A Guideline for Virtual Team Managers: The Key to Effective Social Interaction and Communication," *Electronic Journal of Information Systems Evaluation* 12 (2009): 109-18.

Jeremy Seligman, "Building a Systems Thinking Culture at Ford Motor Company," *Reflections* 6 (2005): 1-9.

Sandhya Shekhar, "Understanding the Virtuality of Virtual

Organizations," *Leadership and Organization Development Journal* 27 (2006): 465-83.

Sandhya Shekhar and L. S. Ganesh, "A Morphological Framework for Virtual Organizations," *IIMB Management Review* (2007): 355-64.

Yuhyung Shin, "A Person-Environment Fit Model for Virtual Organizations," *Journal of Management* 30 (2004): 725-43.

Frank Siebdrat, Martin Hoegl, and Holger Ernst, "How to Manage Virtual Teams," *MIT Sloan Management Review* 50 (2009): 63-68.

Aelita Skaržauskienė, "Theoretical Insights to Leadership Based on Systems Thinking Principles," *Management of Organizations: Systematic Research* 48 (2008): 105-20.

Florence Stone, "Molson Coors 'Our Brew,'" *MWorld* 9 (2010): 16-19.

David C. Strubler and Benjamin W. Redekop, "Entrepreneurial Human Resource Leadership: A Conversation with Dwight Carlson," *Human Resource Management* 49 (2010): 793-804.

The Telework Advisory Group of WorldatWork, "Exploring Telework as a Business Continuity Strategy: A Guide to Getting Started," 2005, http://www.workingfromanywhere.org/news/ ITAC_Explore_Telework.pdf.

The Telework Advisory Group of WorldatWork, "Telework Trendlines 2009," February 2009, www.worldatwork.org/waw/ adimLink?id=31115.

Akio Toyoda, testimony to U.S. House Committee on Oversight and Government Reform, February 24, 2010.

Marianne van Woerkom and Karin Sanders, "The Romance of Learning from Disagreement: The Effect of Cohesiveness and Disagreement on Knowledge Sharing Behavior and Individual Performance within Teams," *Journal of Business and Psychology* 25 (2010): 139-49.

"Virtual Competition," *Economist* 388 (2008): 78.

"'Visible' Innovation," *Quality* 72 (July 2007).

Robin L. Wakefield, Dorothy E. Leidner, and Gary Garrison, "A
  Model of Conflict, Leadership, and Performance in Virtual
  Teams," *Information Systems Research* 19 (2008): 434-55.

Yung-Shui Wang and Tung-Chun Huang, "The Relationship of
  Transformational Leadership with Group Cohesiveness and
  Emotional Intelligence," *Social Behavior and Personality: An
  International Journal* 37 (2009): 379-92.

J. Webster and W. K. P. Wong, "Comparing Traditional and Virtual
  Group Forms: Identity, Communication and Trust in Naturally
  Occurring Project Teams," *The International Journal of Human
  Resource Management* 19 (2008): 41-62.

Hein Wendt, Martin C. Euwema, and I. J. Hetty van Emmerik,
  "Leadership and Team Cohesiveness across Cultures," *Leadership
  Quarterly* 20 (2009): 358-70.

Patricia Werhane, "Mental Models, Moral Imagination and System
  Thinking in the Age of Globalization," *Journal of Business Ethics* 78
  (2008): 463-74.

John Whiteoak, "The Relationship Among Group Process
  Perceptions, Goal Commitment and Turnover Intention in Small
  Committee Groups," *Journal of Business and Psychology* 22 (2007):
  11-20.

INDEX

ABOUT THE AUTHOR

Dr. Marta Wilson is founder and CEO of Transformation Systems, Inc. (TSI) and leads TSI's dynamic group of PhDs and possibility thinkers to help executives achieve bold enterprise transformation goals. Wilson represents TSI in the business community as a thought leader and innovator in the field of organizational excellence. She holds a PhD in industrial and organizational psychology from Virginia Tech and authors leadership articles and books, including Leaders in Motion, The Transformation Desktop Guide, and Live a Difference. Wilson also steers TSI's corporate social responsibility program, Feed to Lead, which nourishes the body, mind and spirit by supporting leadership potential in those who need a helping hand. Whether drawing on her own experience or that of the many leaders she has interviewed, Wilson helps the reader become a leader who is committed to making every thought, word and deed count.

TRANSFORMATION SYSTEMS, INC.

Founded in 2002 by Dr. Marta Wilson, Transformation Systems, Inc. (TSI) is a woman-owned small business headquartered in Arlington, VA with bases of operation in Washington, DC, Stafford, VA, and Warren, MI. Time and time again, TSI has proven to be on target while enthusiastically exceeding customer expectations and building a track record of outcomes including significant cost reductions and exceptional revenue leaps.

Recognized by clients as the source for world-class workplace transformation solutions, TSI helps leaders achieve their audacious goals for a faster, better and smarter organization. Executives seek assistance from TSI's interdisciplinary team of experts whose advanced credentials and experience in engineering, psychology, business and evaluation provide the edge to catalyze positive change and solve complex problems while achieving measurable and sustainable success.

TSI offers consultative services in organizational change facilitation; strategic and implementation planning; professional development training; leadership coaching; and comprehensive results measurement.

Wilson has written, "As the founder of TSI, I serve as a leader among my valued colleagues, all of whom are experts in transformation. We are regularly invited to overhaul performance on individual, group and organizational levels. How do we do this? We do it by keeping leaders in motion."

For more information about TSI, please visit
www.transformationsystems.com